ENJOYING

WISLEY'S BIRDS

FEATURING THE VILLAGE AND THE
ROYAL HORTICULTURAL SOCIETY GARDEN

DAVID ELLIOTT   JUNE ELLIOTT

CHRIS HOWKINS

FIRST PUBLISHED 1988

RESEARCHED AND WRITTEN BY

David Elliott and
June Elliott

ILLUSTRATED AND EDITED BY

Chris Howkins

COPYRIGHT 1988 ©

TEXT : David Elliott
        June Elliott
        Chris Howkins

ILLUSTRATIONS : Chris Howkins

PRINTED IN ENGLAND BY

Unwin Brothers Limited,
The Gresham Press,
Old Woking,
Surrey. GU22 9LH

Tufted Duck

PUBLISHED BY
Chris Howkins, 70, Grange Road,
New Haw, Weybridge, Surrey, KT15 3RH

ISBN 0 9509105 3 8

2

Contents

Introduction   4
Maps   6
Habitats   9
Nesting Boxes   20
Ringing   23

Most Regularly
    Recorded Species   31

Rarities and
    Birds from the Past   181

Index   191

Introduction

What to look for,

Where to look

When to look.......

        ....Those are the three main
objectives of this book. Every year over half
a million people come to Wisley to enjoy the
marvellous range of plants being grown in the
Garden of the Royal Horticultural Society. All
around them in this small corner of Surrey is
a wealth of wildlife equally rich. It's the
birds that attract most attention with over
seventy species being recorded in a good year.
Even on a day's visit up to forty species is a
possibility.
        Since the Royal Horticultural
Society took over the Garden in 1904 the birdlife has been a continuing source of interest,
so that we have been able to draw upon records
going back to those very first years. In 1909
a list of some 74 species was published as then
being present in the Garden. By 1947 the
Society for the Promotion of Field Studies had
started a detailed survey, followed in 1949 by
the London Natural History Society whose
members recorded 79 species. Many were different
from those on the 1909 list. Then in 1955 a
list of 113 species was produced of which 101
were present at that time.

        The next 25 years brings a break in the
records until, in 1982, the then Director of
the Garden and his wife asked us to survey the
situation again. After six years and much
co-operation from many people, the results are
now published as this volume. The total list
is now 144 of which about a dozen species are
unlikely to be recorded again and many others
are now rare visitors to Wisley. Nevertheless
about 90 species could occur annually.

        These are grouped into 87 extended entries
with the rarer birds listed separately in a
second section. They are listed in their
scientific order with an alphabetical index at
the end. These lists are not necessarily
complete as they rely upon people making known
their observations. Some are handed in at the
RHS Information Centre, some are published by
other organizations and these are credited in
the text where appropriate while the local
people have been very helpful in passing on
material directly to us.

courtship

The illustrations have been chosen to match the notes. They record the birds as seen in the field rather than displaying their individual characteristics as in books designed for identification. Material has been selected from the artist's sketchbooks and previous publications to which has been added an extensive new range for which the details were taken from the writers' personal collection of photographs. Thus a whole range of studies has been included, from field jottings to larger sketches and more detailed drawings. The whole survey has been presented informally in the hope that it will encourage visitors to Wisley to note and sketch their sightings ready for the next time Wisley birdlife is surveyed.

D.I.F.ELLIOTT

J.H.ELLIOTT

C.D.HOWKINS

ACKNOWLEDGEMENTS

We should like to thank Mr.C.D.Brickell, Director General of the Royal Horticultural Society, and his wife, for their encouragement to embark upon this survey and to thank Mr.B.M.C.Ambrose, Managing Director of RHS Enterprises Ltd., for bringing the team together and offering his valued guidance.

We should also like to thank all the bird watchers, visitors to the Garden, the villagers of Wisley and other friends who so generously shared their knowledge for this book.

Also much appreciated was the help given by local fifth formers with preparing the final manuscript for print. Finally we should like to thank the staff of Unwin Brothers Ltd., for all their personal service, patience and care with the printing of "Enjoying Wisley's Birds".

ADDITIONAL SOURCES

RHS Garden Club Journals
Surrey Bird Reports
British Birds

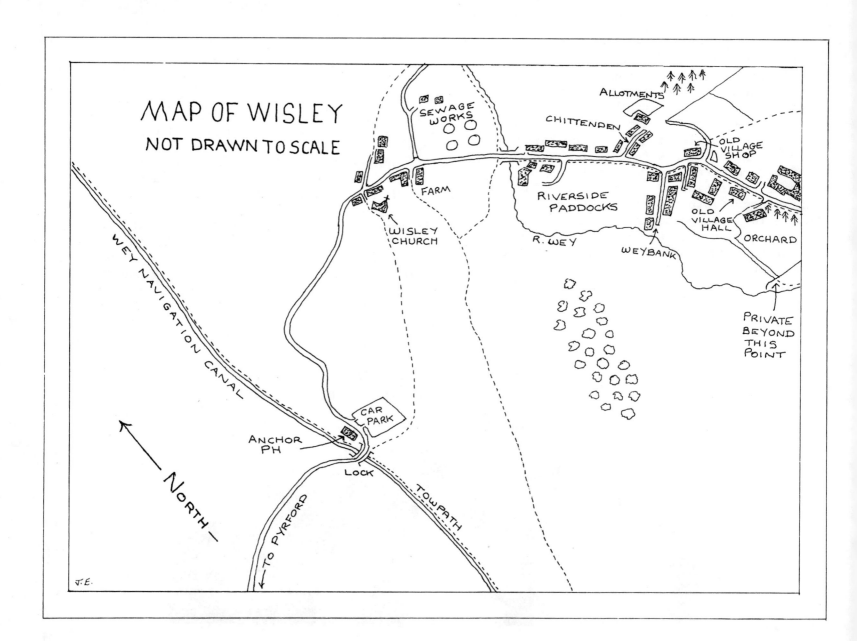

MAP OF WISLEY

NOT DRAWN TO SCALE

SEWAGE WORKS

ALLOTMENTS

CHITTENDEN

OLD VILLAGE SHOP

FARM

RIVERSIDE PADDOCKS

OLD VILLAGE HALL

ORCHARD

WISLEY CHURCH

R. WEY

WEYBANK

PRIVATE BEYOND THIS POINT

WEY NAVIGATION CANAL

North —

CAR PARK

ANCHOR PH

LOCK

TO PYRFORD

TOWPATH

J.E.

6

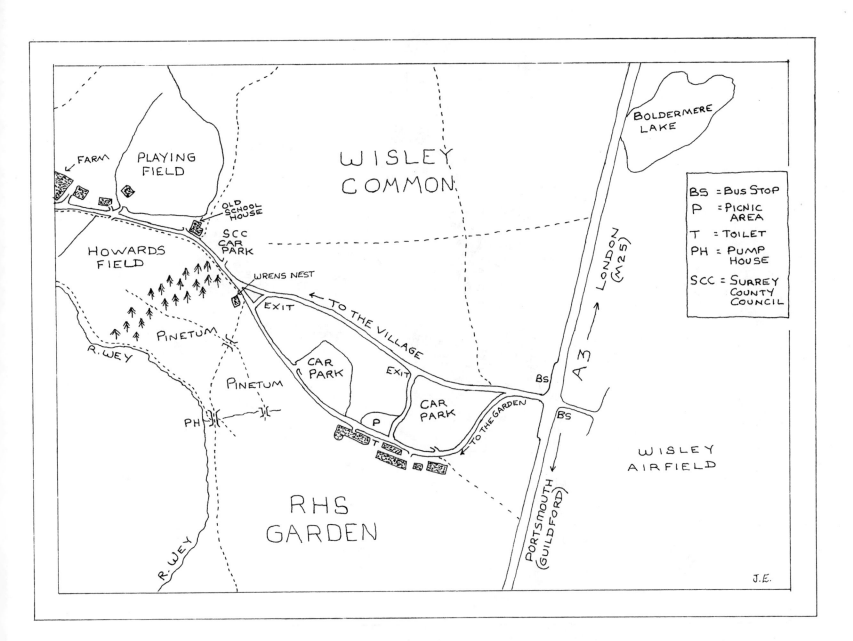

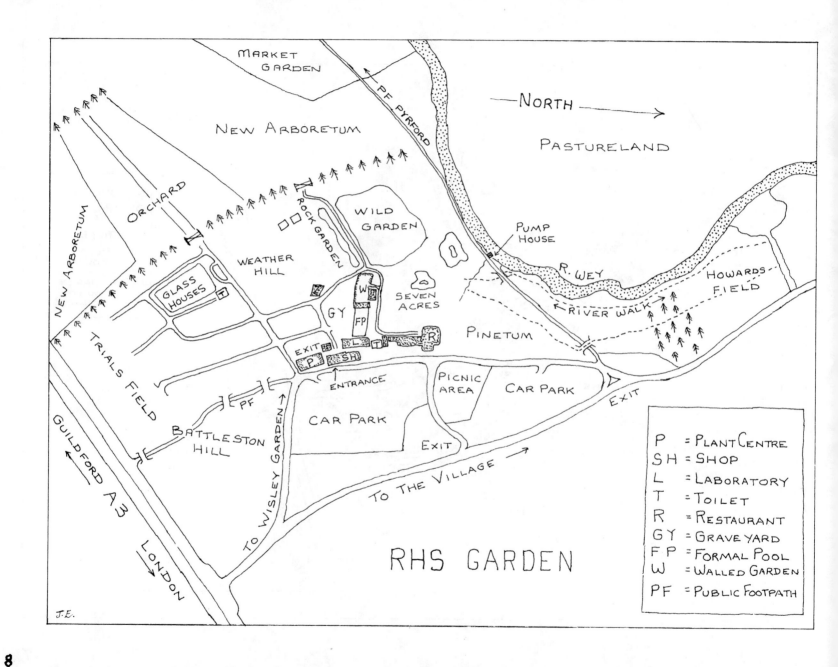

RHS GARDEN

P	=	PLANT CENTRE
SH	=	SHOP
L	=	LABORATORY
T	=	TOILET
R	=	RESTAURANT
GY	=	GRAVE YARD
FP	=	FORMAL POOL
W	=	WALLED GARDEN
PF	=	PUBLIC FOOTPATH

MARKET GARDEN

PF PYRFORD

NORTH

PASTURELAND

NEW ARBORETUM

ORCHARD

NEW ARBORETUM

WILD GARDEN

ROCK GARDEN

PUMP HOUSE

R. WEY

HOWARDS FIELD

WEATHER HILL

GLASS HOUSES

SEVEN ACRES

RIVER WALK

GY

FP

W

TRIALS FIELD

EXIT

L

T

R

PINETUM

P

SH

ENTRANCE

PF

PICNIC AREA

CAR PARK

EXIT

BATTLESTON HILL

CAR PARK

EXIT

GUILDFORD A3

LONDON

TO WISLEY GARDEN

TO THE VILLAGE

J.E.

The Habitats

Goldcrest country - RHS Pinetum.

9

Boldermere

The Common

Boldermere, beside the A3 London to Portsmouth Road, is the largest expanse of open water to attract birds. It has aquatic plants including water lilies, marginal plants and a good sheltering surround of trees, both coniferous and broadleaved.

It is becoming an increasingly popular tourist spot and is very disturbed by anglers, windsurfers and even skaters when it is iced over. Despite this it is still worth a visit, especially at quiet times, with Canada Geese, Mallard, Moorhens and Coots nesting. In the winter a much wider range of waterfowl make occasional visits to rest and feed but their stay is often of very short duration and they can be easily missed. Closer observation could well add considerably to our knowledge of the bird life of Wisley.

ACCESS

Adequate car parking is now provided from the southbound carriageway of the A3. For northbound motorists and those turning out of Wisley Lane there is a roundabout to the north by which the southbound carriageway can be reached. There is a footbridge for pedestrians.

Wisley's common is a very varied and therefore a very interesting habitat. Much of it is dry grassland merging into heathland and that into birch scrub, pines and then mixed woodland. This is Tree Pipit country, with the trees providing song posts and the tussocky grass good nesting sites. Other parts of the common remain flooded after wet weather and where there are pools it's always worth checking for waterfowl and waders, especially in winter. On the whole, the most rewarding times to visit are in the spring and summer; then you can enjoy evenings with the Tree Pipits singing, the Woodcock roding and just possibly the weird song of the Nightjar as night falls. Unfortunately you'll also hear the M25.

The common has a good range of the more familiar birds, some rarer ones too and is the only Wisley location for some species.

ACCESS

Various access points along Wisley Lane from the A3 to the start of the village. A good point is from the Old School House which takes in some interesting woodland before the common. By keeping right along the path it is possible to complete a circular walk.

NOTICE : There are adders on the common.
         DO NOT HARM THEM.

The Farmland

The farmland in the Wisley area is almost exclusively pasture of varying quality with the exception of the Market Gardens bordering the New Arboretum in the RHS Garden. The largest single area is that opposite the Garden, which is cut regularly for hay or silage and thus kept low. For this reason and for the lack of hedging it is almost devoid of breeding birds.

Any flooding in autumn attracts large numbers of Gulls with their accompanying Pipits and Wagtails. In early summer when the silage is cut it is the turn of the Starlings to be attracted by the newly available supply of invertebrate food at just the time when the young have recently fledged.

The rest of the farmland, particularly to the canal or west side is mostly rough pasture with hedging and thus much more attractive to birds. Warblers nest in the hedges and Skylarks out in the fields, together with Reed Buntings towards the water and Yellowhammers towards the hedges. Lapwing and Snipe have both nested on occasions and are present in autumn and winter when flooding adds to the attractiveness to waders and sometimes waterfowl.

ACCESS

The farmland is PRIVATE so keep to the footpaths, keep dogs under control and cause no damage.

FOOTPATHS

1) From the farm near the church which can also be joined where Wisley Lane crosses the river. It eventually joins the canal towpath near Pyrford Place – turn right to return to Wisley Lane.
2) From Wisley Church to The Anchor Public House where you can join Footpath 1.
3) From the house called the "Wren's Nest" in Wisley Lane through to Ripley from where you can return along the towpath to The Anchor.
4) From the back of the Old Village Shop across to Byfleet.

Looking into the farm from Wisley Lane, by the church.

Farmland was the scene recorded at Wisley for the Doomsday Book
in 1086 and this present successor maintains the traditional
land use, ensuring pastures rather than housing and providing a
wide range of habitats and seasonal activities for birds to exploit.

12

View from Wisley Churchyard.

The traditional farm buildings and muddy yard
provide nesting and roosting places, seedy weeds
for food, soft mud to probe for worms or to
build nests with - a varied habitat for birdlife.

The RHS Garden

The Sewage Works

The area of the RHS Garden suits the widest range of species at Wisley because it is so varied. There are artificial habitats like the glasshouses which attract Blackbirds, Pied Wagtails and other 'garden' species; orchards which attract the wintering thrushes; ornamental waters for Mallard and Moorhens. Then there are the more natural habitats like the woodlands thick with brambles suiting Blackcap and Garden Warbler; the riverbank with nesting Kingfishers; grassland and hedgerows in the New Arboretum for Grey Partridge and Whitethroat.

From the wide lawns it's possible to view great expanses of sky to note passing Gulls and Cormorants etc. A few species, such as the Tawny Owl, are not likely to be noticeable during the Garden's open hours and are much more difficult for the visitor to record yet even the Tawny Owl sometimes yields a hoot or two during daylight hours.

With patience and luck a total of some forty species can be recorded on a full day's bird watching in the Garden.

ACCESS
By payment at the main entrance except for members of the Royal Horticultural Society. Members only, on Sundays, from 1988.

This small site beside Wisley Lane is an excellent spot to watch although not as rewarding as some of the other local sewage works. Increased observation would quite probably add some of the species, particularly the waders, which occur elsewhere locally but not, so far, at Wisley.

The site has three attractions, apart from enjoying privacy from human disturbance. The filter beds themselves provide rich pickings for flocks of Gulls and Starlings. The surrounding rough grassland helps to attract Wagtails and Pipits and when it runs to seed, good sized flocks of Finches and Buntings, including Brambling and Tree Sparrow in the autumn. Thirdly, there are areas of thick scrub appreciated by the Warblers.

ACCESS
Strictly prohibited but the site can be viewed from the footpaths along the northern and southern boundaries.

Along the Village Street

The village houses are strung along Wisley Lane and attract species not so regularly seen in other parts of the area. Even some of our common garden birds will not be so common to visitors from other parts of the country.

Starting at the eastern end, the windbreak at the end of the RHS Garden is the first site of note as this is much frequented by Greenfinches and they can be regularly seen flying across to the trees bordering the sports field.

By the Old Village Shop is a likely place to seek Collared Doves which come to feed in the chicken run. They nest in the trees around the old farm at the western end.

Behind the houses of Chittenden are the village allotments. Not all of these are in use at present and so the seeding weeds attract flocks of Finches.

On the other side of the lane, between the houses and the river are a series of paddocks where in milder weather a good range of thrushes come to feed. In severe weather they are more likely to be found in the RHS Orchards.

Beyond the sewage works are the farm buildings attracting Collared Doves, Sparrows and Starlings. Here, in summer, come the House Martins to collect mud with which to build their nests.

Of great importance in the village are the small private gardens, attracting Tits, House Sparrows, Starlings, Dunnocks etc. Less expected perhaps are appearances by all three species of Woodpecker, while those gardens that have ponds attract both Pied and Grey Wagtail.

Many households provide food for the birds in the winter and increase the range of species considerably. These include Greenfinch, Siskin, Nuthatch, Goldcrest and Reed Bunting. Congregations of such birds around a bird table also draw the attention of the Sparrowhawk, looking for an easy meal.

ACCESS

Birds can be watched all along Wisley Lane but please remember that the adjoining properties are all private and their privacy should not be intruded upon.

Waterways

cygnet

There are two main waterways in the Wisley area. One is the River Wey proper and the other is a 17thC. canal to shorten it, known as the River Wey Navigation.

As the River Wey runs in a north/south direction it is ideally suited as a migration route and brings through Wisley several species which might not otherwise have been recorded.

It cuts deeply into the soft soil, producing high sandy banks, used in the past by Sand Martins and still used by the several pairs of Kingfisher. It also leaves sand bars on which the waterfowl rest and on which the Sandpipers rest and feed before continuing their migration.

These high banks prevent the growth of lush thickets of waterside vegetation, such as reed beds, although there are indications that reed beds did once flourish. Without them there is little to attract many Reed and Sedge Warblers. Instead there are borders of brambles or, where the river cuts through pasture, lush grassland. Here the waterfowl nest - at least one pair of Mute Swans, several pairs of Canada Geese, even more Mallard, not to mention such birds as the Grey Wagtail which can usually be seen along the stretch by the sewage works. Mandarin also frequent the river on some occasions. It is all becoming a more valuable habitat as a refuge from the disturbance at Boldermere and RHS Garden lakes.

The river is also important to those species driven to seek running water when still waters ice over in the winter. Thus to Wisley come, occasionally, species off the London reservoirs that would otherwise occur far less frequently in the local records.

The alder trees along both the river and the canal become important feeding sites for both Siskin and Redpoll between November and March.

The canal is far less attractive than the river to waterfowl as it is too disturbed and there is less marginal cover. Nevertheless the Wisley stretch of the towpath is one of several rewarding locations along its $19\frac{1}{2}$ mls.

ACCESS
Best locations:
1) the riverside walk in the RHS Garden,
2) the footpath from Wisley to Ripley follows a short section of the river; path begins at the "Wren's Nest" in Wisley Lane,
3) the footpath from Wisley to Byfleet; starts beside the sewage works,
4) canal towpath; join at The Anchor.

Woodland

Quite an extensive part of the Wisley area is still woodland, with both deciduous and evergreen trees. The latter consists mainly of pine, bordering the common and again at Boldermere at the junction of the A3 and the M25. These are the best places for Goldcrests and Coal Tits and during their invasion years - the Crossbill.

The deciduous woodland is the more extensive, consisting mainly of mature oak with much birch bordering the common. The other important species, occurring in reasonable numbers, is the alder, attracting Siskins and Redpolls in the autumn and winter.

All the woodland is worth a visit at any season of the year. It holds all three species of woodpecker which are at their most visible in the winter which is also the best time for a chance sighting of the Hawfinch. Come in the summer and the woodlands are rich with warblers, especially where there is thick bramble undergrowth. Here you'll find Blackcap and Garden Warbler, Chiffchaff and Willow Warbler and with the undergrowth persisting there's still the hope of the Nightingale returning as a breeding species. Woodcock may also be flushed up but are better seen when roding on the common.

ACCESS

There are a number of places about Wisley where you can walk off through trees or at least look for woodland birds.

For a short walk the best location is at the Old School House where you walk towards the common through good mixed woodland.

For a longer walk try following the footpath from the back of the Old Village Shop which gives access to the woodland beyond the M25.

Varied Habitats of the
R.H.S. Garden.
1973

19

Blackbird defeats
the object and
builds on top of
a box intended
for Blue Tits !
1987.

Nesting Boxes in the RHS Garden

Since the very early days
of the Garden there has been
an interest in its birdlife,
reflected in the provision
of nesting boxes to foster
the breeding species.

Boxes for Blue Tits and Great
Tits were soon installed in the
Wild Garden and in the 1909
report was recorded their use
by Wrynecks. That species
has dramatically declined
but there are still a number
of places in the Garden today
where nesting boxes are
provided and used.

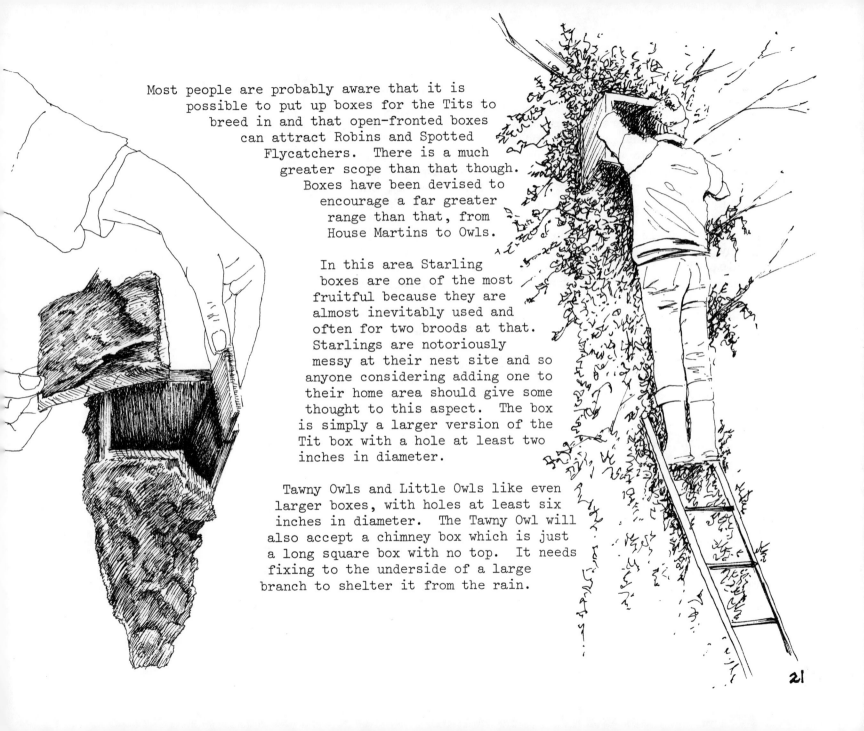

Most people are probably aware that it is
possible to put up boxes for the Tits to
breed in and that open-fronted boxes
can attract Robins and Spotted
Flycatchers. There is a much
greater scope than that though.
Boxes have been devised to
encourage a far greater
range than that, from
House Martins to Owls.

In this area Starling
boxes are one of the most
fruitful because they are
almost inevitably used and
often for two broods at that.
Starlings are notoriously
messy at their nest site and so
anyone considering adding one to
their home area should give some
thought to this aspect. The box
is simply a larger version of the
Tit box with a hole at least two
inches in diameter.

Tawny Owls and Little Owls like even
larger boxes, with holes at least six
inches in diameter. The Tawny Owl will
also accept a chimney box which is just
a long square box with no top. It needs
fixing to the underside of a large
branch to shelter it from the rain.

21

Owl boxes with the large hole might be taken
over by Stock Doves or by Jackdaws. In the case of
the Jackdaw quite large colonies can be encouraged
in an area where there are already a few pairs present.
At Wisley the boxes provided specially for the Jackdaws
are not proving as attractive as was hoped. They seem
to prefer natural holes and there are enough of those
for the needs of the present population. However, the
boxes are not wasted; they have been adopted by Tawny
Owls for roosting in.
    Boxes should not be taken down during the winter
as many birds will shelter in them. Numerous Wrens, for
example, will all pile into one Tit box to benefit not
only from its shelter but from their own communal warmth.

    The enlarged type of Tit box, with a five inch hole,
has proved successful with Mandarin ducks - the only
tree-breeding duck found around Wisley. The box provided
for them by the river was ignored although the Mandarins
bred nearby. In the Great Gale of October 16th/17th 1987
this box was destroyed but replacements are planned.
Stock Doves and Jackdaws will adopt a Mandarin box.

    The final type of box used at Wisley at present is one
for Treecreepers which is wedge-shaped with a corner cut
away to provide an entrance. This odd design is to trick
the bird into thinking it's a piece of bark falling away
from the tree, which is its natural nest site. To add to the
deception, tree bark is fixed over the outside, preferably of
the same type as the tree onto which the box is to be fixed.

    Always fix boxes very securely, including the lids to
stop squirrels getting at the eggs or young. If you spot
any of the boxes around Wisley please do not disturb them.

Owl box in
Wild Garden.

Ringing at
Wisley

23

Catching the birds in a net worries some people too. Hopefully the following notes will be reassuring. Anyone new to ringing is likely to be disturbed by the warning that some species shriek to their fellows when they are handled. Remember, the shrieks are designed to be disturbing and are part of the bird's defence strategy, hoping it will startle the enemy into releasing it. The volume released by a young jay is quite astounding, but loud abuse is a good healthy sign ! It's only used by certain species.

Of the two methods of catching birds used at Wisley the main one is with a mist net. It consists of fine 1.25 in. nylon mesh tethered in such a way that shelves are created from which netting hangs as a loose bag. Being very fine and black in colour, it is almost invisible when erected against a dark background.

Being almost invisible, the birds fly into it and drop down from one of the shelves into the bag of slack net. From there it is very quickly retrieved by the ringer.

That is the stage recorded in this illustration. The Great Tit was not left there all the time it would take to draw it but was quickly photographed by the author and the drawing made from that.

The bird is then lifted very carefully from the net so as not to frighten it unduly or to damage any of its feathering. While this is being done the ringer is also ensuring that the species has been identified correctly. The bird is held in the "ringers' grip" which supports the weight and prevents it from struggling which might otherwise damage or exhaust it.

24

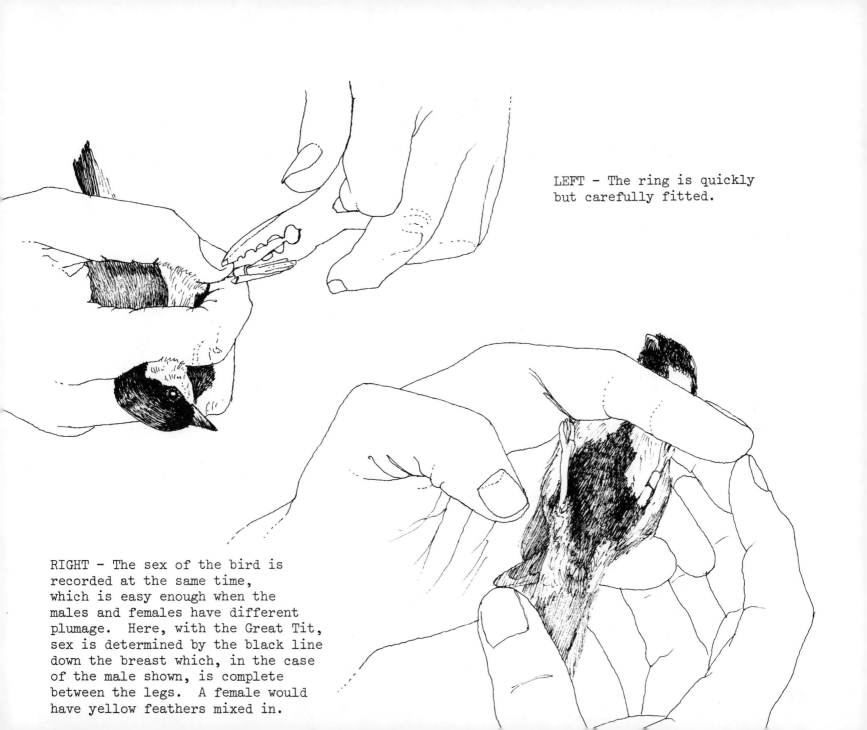

LEFT - The ring is quickly but carefully fitted.

RIGHT - The sex of the bird is recorded at the same time, which is easy enough when the males and females have different plumage. Here, with the Great Tit, sex is determined by the black line down the breast which, in the case of the male shown, is complete between the legs. A female would have yellow feathers mixed in.

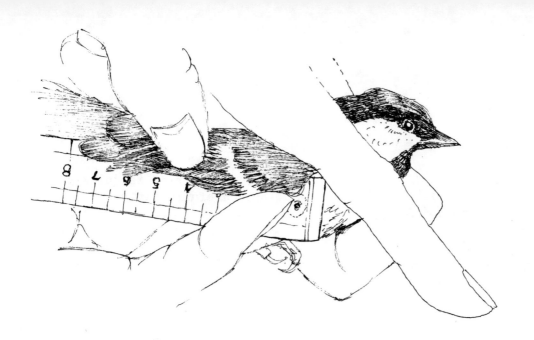

ABOVE - The birds have their wing length
measured in millimetres. The Great Tit
should be c.75 mm.depending upon sex.

RIGHT - Finally the birds are weighed in
grammes. The Great Tit would be about
20 g. The cup is specially designed to
hold the bird safely and comfortably.

All this sounds very time consuming
but is done very quickly so that the
bird is liberated as soon as possible.

No cruelty was involved in making these
illustrations; they were drawn from
photographs.

Some birds are not only born at Wisley but spend all their lives there. Others are migratory, perhaps returning to Wisley each year, perhaps not. Other species just pass through on their travels.

This knowledge comes largely from the information gained by ringing the birds. Without doing that we would know so little about bird movements and without that knowledge our efforts at conservation could so easily be misdirected and ineffective.

Ringing involves placing an aluminium ring around a bird's leg. All the rings are individually numbered so each ring is unique and if ever retrieved can be traced back in the records to the time and place of ringing. The British Museum acts as the centre for this and anyone finding a dead bird that has a ring is asked to notify the British Museum of the number, the date found and the location. In return the finder receives a print-out giving details of where and when the bird had been ringed. Every return adds to our pattern of knowledge.
Additionally, information is also gained by ringers catching a bird already ringed.

Some people naturally question whether ringing is in any way harmful to the bird. Every precaution is taken to ensure that it is not. Ringing is only permitted under licence from the Nature Conservancy and the British Trust for Ornithology, by dedicated people who have undergone several years of training before being qualified to ring unsupervised. The rings themselves are designed to fit so as not to cause discomfort, danger nor hinderance. Thus they are graded according to leg sizes. The tool used to fix them is specially designed to prevent a ring closing onto a leg rather than round it.

The longevity records for individual species speak for themselves - 27 years for an Arctic Tern, 21 years for a Swift and 16 years for a Swallow. These three examples are all long distance migrants too, enduring the greatest strain yet carrying a ring. If the Swallow covered 6000 miles on each migration it clocked up a staggering 92 000 miles not including all the miles covered in between times while hawking for airborne insects.

27

The second method of ringing birds used at Wisley is to simply ring the nestlings in their nest. This is obviously much simpler than using mist nets and has the advantage that if any are recovered later then their exact age will be known.

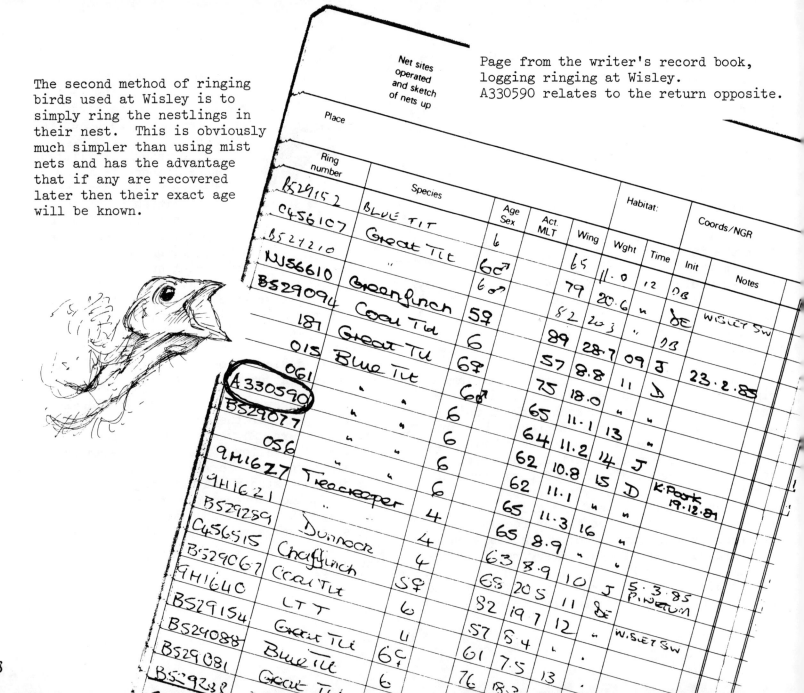

Page from the writer's record book, logging ringing at Wisley. A330590 relates to the return opposite.

Ring number	Species	Age Sex	Act. MLT	Wing	Wght	Time	Init	Notes
B529152	BLUE TIT							
C456107	Great Tit	6						
B529210	"	6♂	65	11.0	12	DB		
NJ56610	Greenfinch	6♂	79	20.6	"	DE	WISLEY SW	
B529094	Coal Tit	5♀	82	20.3	"	DB		
187	Great Tit	6	89	28.7	09	J		
015	Blue Tit	6♀	57	8.8	11	D	23.2.85	
061	"	6♂	75	18.0	"			
A330590	"	6	65	11.1	13	"		
B529077	"	6	64	11.2	14	J		
056	"	6	62	10.8	15	D	K.Pork 19.12.84	
9H1627	Treecreeper	6	62	11.1	"	"		
9H1621	"	4	65	11.3	16	"		
B529289	Dunnock	4	65	8.9	"	"		
C456515	Chaffinch	4	63	8.9	10	J	5.3.85 PINETUM	
B529067	Coal Tit	5♀	63	20.5	11	DE		
9H1640	L T T	6	82	19.7	12	"	W.SLEY SW	
B529154	Great Tit	4	57	5.4	"	"		
B529088	Blue Tit	6♀	61	7.5	13	"		
B529081	Great Tit	6	76	8.7				
B529288								

Net sites operated and sketch of nets up

Place

Habitat:

Coords/NGR

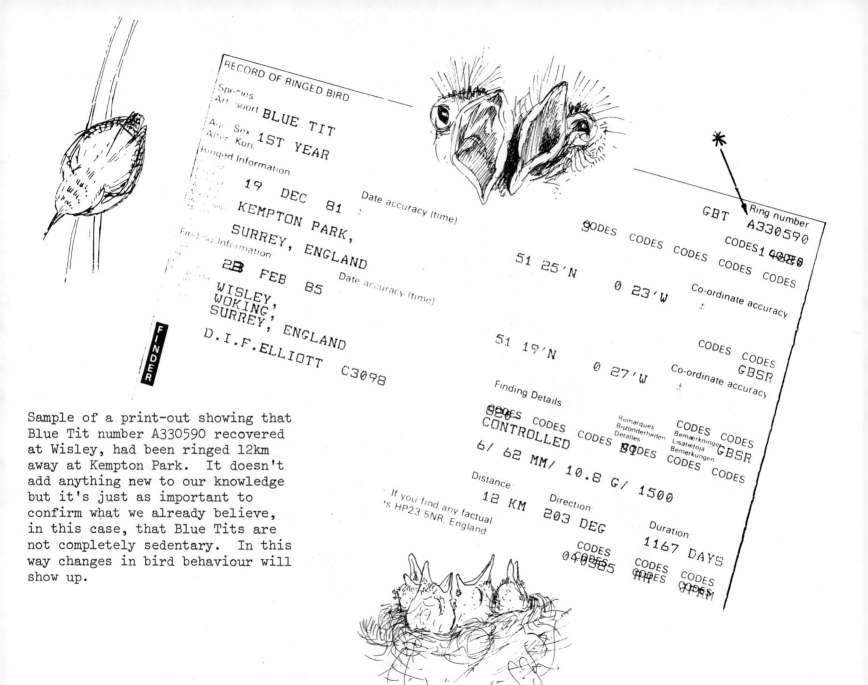

RECORD OF RINGED BIRD

Species
Art soort **BLUE TIT**

Age Sex
Alter Kon. **1ST YEAR**

Ringed Information

19 DEC 81

Date accuracy (time)

KEMPTON PARK,
SURREY, ENGLAND

Finding Information

28 FEB 85

Date accuracy (time)

WISLEY,
WOKING,
SURREY, ENGLAND

D.I.F.ELLIOTT C3098

FINDER

GBT **A330590**
Ring number

CODES CODES CODES CODES CODES CODES1 CODE0

51 25'N   0 23'W
Co-ordinate accuracy
±

51 19'N   0 27'W
Co-ordinate accuracy
±

CODES   CODES
GBSR

Finding Details

CODES CODES CODES CODES CODES
CONTROLLED BY

Remarques
Bijzonderheden
Detalles
Lisätietoja
Bemerkungen

Bemaerkninger

CODES CODES
GBSR
CODES CODES

6/ 62 MM/ 10.8 G/ 1500

Distance
12 KM

Direction
203 DEG

If you find any factual
's HP23 5NR, England

Duration
1167 DAYS

CODES
040385   CODES CODES

Sample of a print-out showing that
Blue Tit number A330590 recovered
at Wisley, had been ringed 12km
away at Kempton Park. It doesn't
add anything new to our knowledge
but it's just as important to
confirm what we already believe,
in this case, that Blue Tits are
not completely sedentary. In this
way changes in bird behaviour will
show up.

29

30

Pied Flycatcher ~ one of the rarer birds at Wisley.

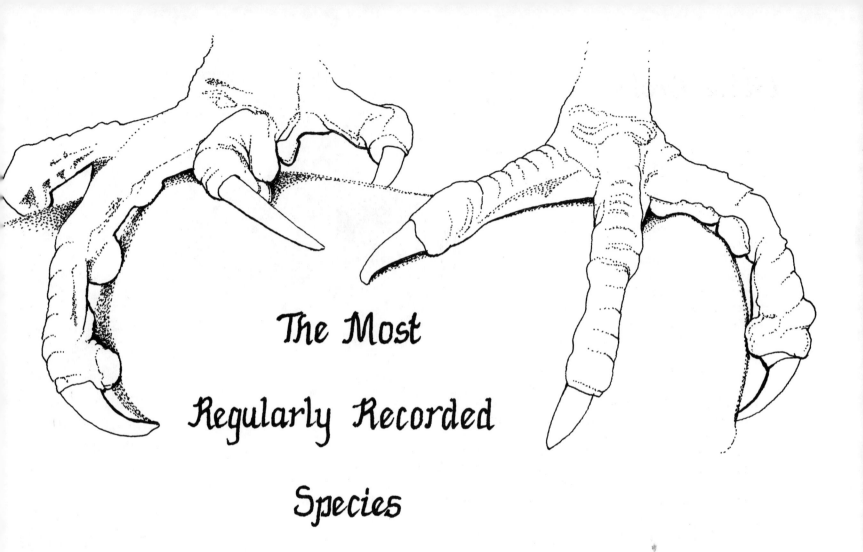

The Most

Regularly Recorded

Species

Little Grebe

The Little Grebe is more widely distributed than the Great Crested Grebe and is far less particular about its breeding sites, accepting quite small ponds providing there is cover and food.

Thus up until 1982 they nested under the willows surrounding the larger of the Seven Acres Lakes in the RHS Garden. There the two young could be watched rushing up to the female each time she surfaced from a dive to the lake bottom for food. Increases in the numbers of visitors to the Garden have proved too disturbing and the Little Grebes have retreated to the comparative peace of the canal and the river. There they can still find the right conditions for breeding. A quiet walk along the Wisley stretches on a summer's evening can still be rewarded by the sight of these small dumpy birds with their young riding on their backs.

They suffer in winter if the water of their habitat freezes over and they cannot reach their aquatic plant food and invertebrates. Then they migrate in search of food, some to the coast, some go abroad.

Great Crested Grebe

Boldermere is the place to seek the Great Crested Grebe because it is wide enough for them to flap and run across the surface to get airborne. It has also been one of the nesting sites in its revival from near extinction last century but with so much summer disturbance is now unlikely to breed here. Marginal disturbance from paddling and picnicking earlier this century was tolerated as the floating nests of weed on the outer fringes of the waterside plants were largely out of reach. The lake centre offered a safe refuge and good vantage point. Nowadays there are no safe havens as swimmers, boaters and windsurfers leave no part undisturbed. Fortunately some of the flooded gravel pits in this part of Surrey have been adopted by the Great Crested Grebe and therefore the possibility of one or more being spotted as visitors to Boldermere is always a possibility, especially in winter. Then large numbers can move into the area to gather on suitable still waters.

Cormorant

Considering that Wisley is nearly forty miles from the sea the possibility of seeing a Cormorant will perhaps surprise some readers. During the breeding season they will indeed be at the coast but between September and March they can be seen flying over on their way between the south coast and the London reservoirs. On the reservoirs they can feed more successfully than in the winter seas. Even that is denied them by ice in severe weather so that's the best time to try and spot one fishing along the ice-free river at Wisley.

Such a sighting would be quite an achievement at Wisley though. More usually they are spotted in flight, not just on the main north/south route but touring local fish farms which are kept ice free. For this they are persecuted by man as they take large valuable fish. In 1986 British trout were valued at £21,228,000 at wholesale level, so depredations by Cormorants are not at all welcome. There are a number of local trout farms as the fish bring a quicker return in southern counties than northern.

The odd name of Cormorant came from the twelth century French. By the fourteenth century Geoffrey Chaucer, who had slight connections with neighbouring Byfleet on the other side of the river, was using 'cormeraunt'. Our neighbours in Kent called it the Coal Goose.

Grey Heron

The ornamental waters in the RHS Garden are stocked with fish and attract hungry herons just like any other garden fish pond. Only the very first of a morning's visitors are likely to see one and then only briefly as it launches itself to safety in the air and beats off on slow rounded wings. Herons don't like people. The alarm call may be given at this time, revealing why the old Surrey name for this bird was 'Frank' or more affectionately, 'Old Frankie'.

A quiet walk along the river when other people are absent may also lead to a sighting. More probably it's one in flight over the district that will be recorded. Their search for food takes them many miles, perhaps from heronries near London or the one in SW Surrey; there isn't one close to Wisley.

The winter is a difficult time for them, especially young inexperienced ones. Some of their prey, such as frogs, are absent for hibernation. The fish move into deeper water and ice may exclude the heron from all. Then moving water becomes more attractive or else they move off to the coast.

Thus Europe's largest heron is a non-breeding 'resident' at Wisley, declining in numbers in line with the national pattern.

Mute Swan

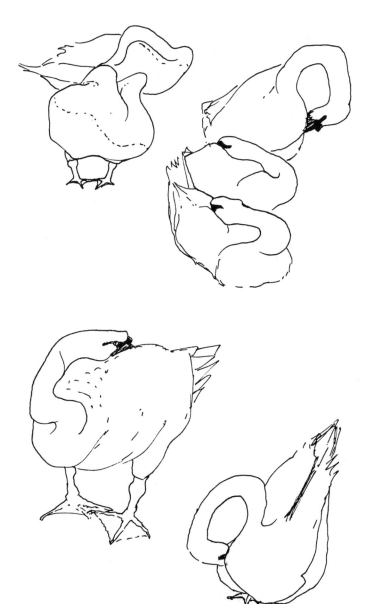

During the review period the Mute Swan has always been part of the Wisley river scene. There have been up to three pairs on the stretch between Pyrford Lock and Byfleet, if one thinks of the canal and the river as one habitat. Here they successfully breed despite all the disturbance from anglers and pleasure boats. Numbers along the Wey have declined in recent years to the point where The National Trust, who own the Wey Navigation, report that there are only twelve pairs left on their twenty mile stretch. Lead poisoning from discarded anglers' weights has been strongly suspected as the main cause. Now that these are being superceded by non-toxic weights it will be interesting to see whether numbers recover.

The Wisley pair have a territory stretching from the Pump House to the far side of the village bridge. Good views are often possible of the cob driving all other birds out of this territory as he patrols in defence of his family. There can be anything up to nine cygnets and these usually stay with the pen, often to be seen in their early days trying to ride on her back. The cob usually follows behind the family group.

The cygnets grow rapidly. Their regular preening place is on the sand bank at the edge of the river below Howards Field.

Readers are warned not to approach the family group too closely and to keep a wary eye on the cob at all times !!!

Canada Goose

This species was one of the specialities of the RHS Garden for some years in the early 1980s when a pair nested at the Seven Acres Lake. All was well until any other goose strayed into the breeding territory of the nesting pair. Then visitors to the Garden were treated to a dramatic display of aggression. The male would lower his head and charge across the lawns with ever increasing vocal honking. This was fine unless his route was obstructed by visitors relaxing in the spring sunshine - then they too had to scatter fast, thereby revealing the full effectiveness of his display !

Such aggression was completely contrasted on other occasions when the visitors to the Garden were able to observe the parental care exercised by the geese. Each day the female would lead her goslings over the grass to the restaurant to scrouge easy food at the same but self-appointed hour each day. For many of the visitors it was a charming and very welcome introduction to the wildlife of Wisley.

The pair in the RHS Garden
have continued to nest and
lay eggs in the last few
years but these have not
reached the stage of hatching.
It does mean though that in
the breeding season, from
March through to May, visitors
who wish to see this bird can
be almost certain of
finding them in the
RHS Garden.

Although breeding success
has fallen in the RHS Garden
a new nesting location has
been established along the
river. It isn't known whether
these birds are the progeny of the
pair in the Garden but two or three
pairs each year have considerable
success at bringing their eggs to hatching
point and then at raising their goslings.
A quiet summer's walk along the river often
gives visitors the chance to see them but
do not stray too close !

Even more frequent
sightings of Canada Geese
are of flocks flying over
the village in their very
characteristic extended V-
formations. Many species
flying overhead are easily missed
but the Canada Geese fly over making
a continuous loud honking.

It is during the winter that the really
big flocks are recorded flying over.
These may contain over 100 birds.
In winter there can be much
movement of flocks as they
search for food, even to the
extent of moving beyond this
country.

This is not a native bird but,
as its name suggests, comes
from North America. It was
introduced as an ornamental
waterfowl back in the time of Charles II and
was recorded breeding freely by 1785. It was
not until after the Second World War that it
expanded so successfully in the wild.

40

Mandarin

It might seem strange in a book about the wild birds of a small area of Surrey, to be including a species with its main area of distribution in the Far East, in China and Japan. Nevertheless, over the past eighty years it has become a breeding resident in the district.

Mandarin were first introduced into wildfowl collections in the early eighteenth century and were breeding in captivity by 1834. For the last fifty years, as a result of escapes and releases, Mandarin have been breeding successfully in the wild, with their main concentration in the Surrey/Berkshire area.

Around Wisley, the Mandarin is generally a spring and summer visitor coming into the area to breed from their wintering grounds. Such grounds, for local birds, may well be in Windsor Great Park where good numbers can be found in winter around Virginia Water.

The illustration may look very odd to some people who do not expect to see a duck in a hole in a tree. That is where they regularly nest though. Mandarin are one of the "perching ducks", the Cairinini. For this reason they have adapted quite well to the special nest boxes provided for them by Surrey birdwatchers. As a result the highly coloured drake and his more subtle grey-brown mate are now quite a regular sight along the river at Wisley. Their presence is often revealed by a low whistling note as they fly away. Breeding was proved in the RHS Gardens in 1985 with the sighting of a female and six small young on the river by the pumphouse. They were not from the box that had been provided nearby and so were more likely to have nested in a natural hole.

Mandarin
drakes

42

Teal

This is a rather under-recorded species. It most often turns up in the winter when birds from the north push south and thousands more pour into Britain from the Continent. Nationally its numbers are on the increase and so sitings at Wisley should increase.

The most likely place to see this small but very attractive duck is along the river or on the local farm fields, especially if there has been flooding. Then weed seeds float to the surface and provide rich pickings for this dabbling duck. In winter some three quarters of its diet consists of seeds.

On one occasion Teal bred on the common which has several wet areas. Teal like the area less since the motorway was built.

Mallard

The Mallard is the other dabbling duck of the Anatini to be found resident at Wisley. It's the most numerous of the wildfowl being found throughout the British Isles wherever there is any expanse of water. Although we know the Mallard in its semi-domesticated state on farm and village ponds, having adapted to living in close proximity to man, in general a good proportion of the population is truly wild. These tend to keep to the more isolated stretches of water away from disturbance. Right round the Northern Hemisphere, from the Arctic Circle down to North Africa it's spread its success.

Numerous pairs frequent the Wisley area throughout the year, particularly along the river and the canal. Even a walk over the common may often result in one being seen, flushed up from one of the isolated patches of water that occur there, especially in winter.

The Mallard's ability to adapt to living in association with man is clearly demonstrated by a pair of truly wild birds breeding at a site where one would not expect to find them - the small island in the middle of the smaller Seven Acres Lake in the RHS Gardens, watched by hundreds of thousands of visitors. Most were unaware of the duck as she incubated her eggs but after hatching, her ten little chicks were a great attraction.

Young mink.
Probably about
6 weeks old.

The second
danger is from
other birds defending their
territory. When the Mallard
ducklings first appeared they were
attacked, and some killed, by the Canada
Geese from the larger adjoining lake.
The aggression continued until the duck
led her chicks across the Garden to the
safety of the small ponds below the Rock
Garden.

The pair also demonstrated two of the
dangers of breeding in even a protected area
like the RHS Gardens. Firstly, that most
ruthless of predators, the mink, posed a
severe threat. This North American carnivore
was introduced into Britain early this century
to be farmed for its fur. Many escaped and
now breed in the wild. The European mink does
not occur in Britain.

Mink are normally territorial and
solitary, hunting by day and by night, even if
there are people about. One of their prime
targets is the waterfowl, including Mallard.

45

Other Waterfowl

Wherever there is a substantial area of water it is quite possible for almost any species to be recorded. It was Boldermere beside the A3 that always drew in the more infrequent visitors but its popularity with birds is declining in proportion to its increased use for human recreation. Some species tolerated this all the time that the centre provided a safe haven but now even that is disturbed as the water increasingly attracts windsurfers.

Aside from the three resident species of Mandarin, Teal and Mallard, records exist for eight other species in the Wisley area.

Of these, the GOOSANDER, representing the Mergini, is at present the most regular visitor. There have been sightings in each of the last few winters along the open water of the river when cold spells have frozen over still waters, especially the London reservoirs.

It is during this sort of weather that the more unusual wildfowl are likely to frequent the river. This was certainly the case with the records of SMEW including one which was shot in the winter of 1954.

It was likewise with four TUFTED DUCK, one drake and three ducks, that were spotted seeking shelter along the riverbank during the cold spell at the beginning of January 1987.

With the exception of GARGANEY which was reported from the common, most of the other records are for Boldermere. These include reports of POCHARD, WIGEON, GADWALL and SHOVELER.

Again, these are usually for the autumn and winter months.

Sparrowhawk

Since the abuse of agricultural chemicals in the 1950s and 60s and the resulting decline in numbers of the birds of prey, there has been a steady recovery back to their former status. Now the sparrowhawk is seen more regularly at Wisley than its more familiar relative, the Kestrel. They almost certainly breed around Wisley but this is difficult to prove due to their secretive nature. They are most often seen simply flying over. Occasionally they can be found hunting where there is a flock of smaller birds feeding, as for instance, at the RHS Fruit Fields. There the sparrowhawk can hide up, under cover, waiting - before flying low and fast out of the bushes to seize its unsuspecting prey. They have also been observed in the winter at the bird tables in the village gardens.

It's the blue tit rather than the sparrow
that is vital to the sparrowhawk.

47

Kestrel

48   Wisley Church ~ favoured Haunt of Kestrels.

For a bird that is nationally as common as the Kestrel it is somewhat surprising that in the Wisley area they are not more regularly seen. For a bird that has adapted to such a wide variety of habitats, from rural countryside to city skyscrapers, there ought to be more than an adequate supply of nest sites around Wisley.

As with the Sparrowhawk they suffered a decline due to pesticide poisoning and also from persecution from gamekeepers. More recently the population appears to have recovered, especially since adopting a lifestyle of feeding along the verges of our main roads and motorways.

This makes the situation at Wisley all the more puzzling, considering that it is at the intersection of two such roads. The verges of the M25 are perhaps too new to support an adequate supply of rodents. There seem to be only enough to support one or two pairs of Kestrels. Their territories are extensive; from Ockham Lane, through the farm fields, over the river and around the church. It was in the vicinity of the church that they bred on at least one occasion. Other likely places to watch for this resident are about the RHS Fruit Fields where they can be watched hovering or else a sharp eye might spot them perched and watching from the trees in Ockham Lane.

49

Red-legged Partridge

This partridge is more likely to be spotted around Wisley than its relative the Grey Partridge because it is less precise in its habitat requirements. The Grey Partridge is very unusual in that it tries to spend all its life in the same couple of fields around the place of its birth. This makes it very vulnerable to changes in agricultural practice. The Red-legged Partridge, on the other hand, is more adaptable and does not restrict itself to farm fields. It will move into the common and even the parts being reclaimed by trees.

Recently at least two broods were reared in the RHS Gardens. The first occurred in the Fruit Fields and the second on Battleston Hill. This second brood numbered at least fifteen and could often be seen hurrying across the car park early in the morning or else strolling as one big family unit up and down the herbaceous borders. One young chick even decided to visit the Information Centre. After causing an hour's hunt it was returned to its family which was eventually located sheltering under a tree near the Plant Centre. Fortunately it was accepted back, with much noise, by the rest of the group.

This is not a native species. First attempts at introducing it were in 1673 but did not succeed until 1790 - in Suffolk. There have been further introductions at regular intervals in order to boost the numbers of this and the native Grey Partridge for shooting. For this purpose another species has also been released in Britain. It's the Chukar and it regularly interbreeds with the Red-legged but as far as is known this has not occurred at Wisley. Anything looking like a Red-legged Partridge is almost certainly that - for the time being.

Grey Partridge

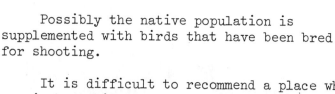

Due to its elusive nature the Grey Partridge is rather an under-recorded species. It is very vulnerable to changes in agriculture because it is so very sedentary, often spending all its life in the same field in which it was born. Some stray into adjoining fields but not very far. Despite changes in agriculture at Wisley, in common with the rest of Surrey, it is still one of Wisley's breeding species, to be found out in the farm fields and in the cover provided by the bases of hedges. It likes solitude without disturbance.

Possibly the native population is supplemented with birds that have been bred for shooting.

It is difficult to recommend a place where one is most likely to see this species but watching around the New Arboretum in the RHS Garden can be rewarding. Here they seek cover whenever there is any shooting in the surrounding fields. Otherwise watching the farmland from cars is more successful than on foot and watching arable land, especially corn fields, is likely to be more rewarding than pasture land.

Pheasant

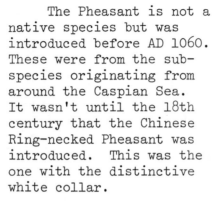

The Pheasant is not a native species but was introduced before AD 1060. These were from the sub-species originating from around the Caspian Sea. It wasn't until the 18th century that the Chinese Ring-necked Pheasant was introduced. This was the one with the distinctive white collar.

Interbreeding between the subspecies has led to much variety in today's stock. Some bear the white collar of the Chinese; some do not.

The local population figures are never stable. In late spring they are boosted with stocks raised by gamekeepers and then the shooting season reduces them again. Many lurk undetected in thick cover, yet the sight of one stalking around the edge of the farm fields is not at all unfamiliar at Wisley. They prefer areas of field that are still within a short run of protective cover if they become alarmed. During the shooting season some retreat to the safety of the RHS Garden.

Moorhen

Wherever there is water the moorhen occurs. This jaunty black and white 'tug boat' chugging low in the water is a firm favourite but non the less interesting for its familiarity. Panic one into flight and it barely leaves the water but thrashes across the surface with long green legs and much wing flapping. Surprisingly then, it is in fact quite a good flier, being a migrant bird in the colder parts of Europe. At Wisley it is a resident all the year round but commoner in the winter when migrant birds from over the North Sea increase British numbers. A further concentration of their numbers arises from birds in the highland parts of Britain moving down into the lowlands for the winter.

54

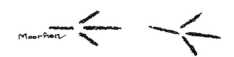

Moorhen

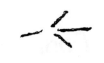

The pair on the smaller lake at Seven Acres in the RHS Garden has been proving that even the familiar can be full of surprises.

On a sunny day in March one was spotted dragging a water lily leaf across the water to the island. Instead of then adding it to a nest near the water line, as might be expected, the bird dragged it up the island and round behind the pine tree that grows there. When it next came into view it was actually climbing the pine tree. Up it continued to climb, in a somewhat ungainly fashion on its long legs, using the branches as a spiral staircase. At about ten feet it moved in towards the fork in the tree trunk. There the mate was spotted with a partly built nest; a most unusual site but not the first such recording.

Very young chicks

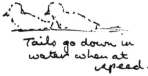

Tails go down in water when at speed.

The water lily leaf was then added to the pile and carefully positioned with much pulling and poking with the bill and just as much treading down with the large feet. The mate, meanwhile, foresook the scene to teeter across to the outer branches from where, with much wing flapping, it plunged to the water below.

Only occasionally are such nests recorded but this pair is making a habit of it. The first egg clutch was taken by a mink but the second that season, and both clutches the following year, were successful. Chicks from the first brood were observed helping to feed those from the second. How delicately the adults tore off small portions of water weed to pass to their tiny young.

At first the young were just tiny black downy bundles but yet quite speedy over the lily pads, outstretching their fin-like wings to keep their balance.

Shoulders very low in water when swimming

Shoulders higher when idling

Coot

The Coot is more fussy than the Moorhen about its habitat, preferring larger expanses of open water, such as wide ponds and lakes. Therefore the most likely place to see it at Wisley is on Boldermere.

Chances of watching them are best in winter when, like the Moorhen, they move to the lower and warmer parts of Britain, increasing the numbers in Surrey. Also like the Moorhen is the tendency to come to Britain from the Continent in the winter. Some come from as far away as Russia. Thus they are better fliers than their boisterous wing-flapping disputes over territory would suggest. The chances of actually seeing them in full flight are rare as they usually move from one water to another during the hours of darkness.

Sometimes they can be seen grazing quite some distance from the water. At Boldermere there is little herbage around so they are more likely to be seen diving to the lake bottom to graze and returning to the surface with the weed before eating it. Although mainly vegetarian, a lot of small animal life will be ingested with the pondweeds. They have also been recorded taking small fish. They will destroy the eggs of other birds and kill ducklings that stray into their territory but these are not eaten.

They prefer still or slow moving water
so the one spotted on the river by
the RHS Garden in July 1987 was
rather unusual, although they
breed on the river near Guildford.
The increase in gravel pits in
Surrey since the 1940s has
suited them well.

Coot and Canada Geese.
1986

Lapwing

The Lapwing or Green Plover
is classified as a wader and of
this group it is the most numerous
and widespread. Nevertheless, sightings
at Wisley are intermittent, as the Lapwing
is declining over Southern Britain.

The reasons for this are being investigated
but the findings are expected to highlight
changes in farming. For thousands of years the
bird has adapted to the older ways of field
management, when there was far less drainage so
that the fields had the wet, often saturated areas,
where it could find food. In the bare patches worn
by cattle it could lay its eggs. When they hatched
there was vegetation nearby in which the young could
hide. As the chicks developed so their diet varied
and this was in line with the sequence of events in
the fields. That's all changed now. For example, wheat
is regularly autumn-sown rather than spring so there's
less bare earth in spring, the wheat is at the wrong
height for hiding in and before the chicks are old enough
to escape, the great harvesters come along and crush them.

59

The day to enjoy them
at Wisley was 19th
January 1969 when flocks of between 97 and 500
were recorded. January is the most likely
time to spot them, when additional flocks
arrive in Britain from northern Europe and
when bad weather forces them to keep on the
move searching for soft unfrozen ground.
Areas gripped in frost and snow are not to
their liking.

Later, during July and August
and in to September they sometimes reappear.
Thus on 30th July 1984 a large flock came to
the field adjacent to the RHS Pinetum, when
it had been freshly cut. The same month
brought flocks again in 1986.

They have also bred at Wisley.
In 1944 and earlier, they were using
the fields next to the RHS Garden.
Even when present in the Spring it is
difficult to prove that they are actually
breeding. The eggs, laid on the ground,
are heavily camouflaged and would prove
exceptionally difficult to find. However,
there was positive confirmation in 1970
and 1971.

Apart from around the farmland
it is also worth looking for them on the
wet areas of the common. They were
frequenting it in 1909 and have continued
to do so. They have also bred there -
confirmed 1971 for example - but their
favourite area was damaged by fire in 1976.

It's also worth watching the skies
for flocks passing over, recognisable by
their rounded slowly beating wings.

Snipe

This shy, resident bird likes soft wet ground, so it finds several localities to its liking at Wisley.

Along the river banks there are a few secluded wet patches from where the Snipe can be flushed occasionally. Chances of seeing them are better in the wet fields bordering the canal and indeed a couple of pairs have nested there. Thirdly, there are a few untended corners left in some of the fields where surface water collects, especially after heavy rain, and these too are exploited by the Snipe for food.

It's a well camouflaged bird at the best of times but in summer when the vegetation is rank it can be even more difficult to spot. It's easier to find in the winter when the vegetation has died down. During frosts the overhanging trees at the corners of some fields keep them from icing up so quickly and here the Snipe can be found feeding. Unfrozen soft soil or mud is essential for in this the Snipe probes with its long bill for food, especially for earthworms. Feeding is a very busy process and rewarding to watch. The bill is stabbed in and out of the ground at an average rate of eight probes a minute. Energy is conserved by standing on the spot and probing in a wide arc around itself before moving its position.

The length of the bill in the
illustration is not exaggerated. It
needs to be that long to enable the
Snipe to probe deep in the ground for
earthworms. Despite being designed
for such rough work the tip of the
bill is sensitive, being the chief
sensor for detecting the prey.
     Small worms and other invertebrates
are sucked straight up and immediately
swallowed but larger prey is dragged to the
surface, hammered senseless and then swallowed
whole.

                    An accurate assessment
              of its breeding at Wisley
              is difficult to achieve
           because the eggs are just as
           well camouflaged as the bird and
           there is no distinctive nest to find
           later; just a scant lining of grass in
        a hollow in the ground. Fortunately the
     Snipe has a noisy mating display which may be
taken as an indicator. This famous "drumming"
sound, which is more like the bleating call
of a sheep, is produced by the wind rushing
through the vibrating tail feathers as the Snipe
plunges downwards during the display flight.
It's now a rare sound through the Wisley fields
but may still be heard out on the common.

Floods under
the alders
at the fields'
edge.
Wisley 1988.

62

Woodcock

Walk through the trees out on the common at dawn or dusk during the breeding season and there's always the chance of hearing, if not seeing, woodcock performing their 'roding' display. This involves them patrolling chosen spaces and woodland rides on slowly beating wings. An odd double croak is uttered, followed by a husky whistle. When roding, two or three birds may come together but otherwise they are our most solitary wader.

Normally this elusive bird roosts by day in a woodland thicket, leaving at dusk to seek wet areas of woodland, common and farmland, to feed. Like the snipe it probes with its long bill for invertebrates, especially for earthworms. It can eat its own weight of these in a day. The tip is slightly swollen with all the nerve endings that make it such an efficient probe. More intriguing is the rare design which enables the tip of the upper mandible to be flexed so that just the worm is gripped, without a beakful of soil.

Although it needs soft ground for feeding, it seeks dry ground for nesting, where it can lay its heavily camouflaged eggs directly into the leaf litter. All these habitats are available at Wisley but Woodcock are so elusive that exact numbers are difficult to assess. Five pairs were recorded on the common in 1984 and six pairs in 1985. The discovery of eggshells confirmed breeding in 1972.

Casual sightings of Woodcock moving between their wet and dry habitats are always possible, sometimes noticed by the whistling flight. Although slow, when roding, the flight can be very fast, especially when it's been flushed out of its roosting thicket.

Woodcock
Black camouflage
patterns.
21·4·-72

65

Common Sandpiper

Crocodiles and hippos provide floating islands in African rivers for this species in winter. In summer the Common Sandpipers have migrated north to bob about the boulders in the fast flowing rivers of the north and west of Britain. To reach these they pass through Wisley. From March to May is a good time to spot them, resting and feeding, either along the River Wey or at the sewage works. By late summer/early autumn they pass through again on their return journey. At this time they are rarely recorded so presumably do not pause for long.

Occasionally a few overwinter and have been recorded (e.g. 28.12.1976). Possibly these are not British but Scandinavian which have migrated as far south as they need. Conversely a few have been known to stay in Surrey for the whole summer. Those that did so in 1969 and 1970 may well have bred.

Common Sandpiper.
Field notebook sketches ~ enlarged
except the smallest.

The Gulls

Traditionally, gulls have been associated with the coast but during this century they've begun moving inland both to feed and to roost. High in the skies over Wisley they've now become a regular sight, following their flight paths from the south coast to the London reservoirs. They still prefer such large expanses of water for roosting, despite having few enemies.

Five species appear in the Wisley records; the lesser and the greater black backed, the herring, the black headed and the common.

Must have gorged itself very heartily to be able to keep its balance at this angle.

Of these the most regular are the herring and the black headed. The former still spends much time at the coast and is normally only recorded on passage over Wisley, increasingl[y] so since the 1920s. The black headed however, will stop to feed on pasture and ploughland, except during the breeding season or when severe winter weather drives them back to the coast. They're also beginning to accept lakes and ponds for roosting.

On shorter cropped pastures during the winter it is also worth looking for the common gull. The sewage works is another likely place to look.

On the arable fields the lesser black backed is more frequent than the herring gull but is still only an occasional winter visitor. It has increased since the 1920s and may be commoner than the records indicate due to the difficulty in identifying gull silhouettes high and tiny in the winter skies.

Much easier to record is the massive great black backed gull scavenging with smaller gulls in the rubbish and sewage. This species has increased steadily since the 1920s from a point nearing extinction at the turn of the century.

Feral Pigeon

Feral pigeons have a worldwide distribution so may well be recognised by any visitor to Wisley. They can be seen throughout the year but it's during the winter that they can be particularly noticeable when they sometimes flock together and come down to feed on weed seeds. This is their old way of life for these are descended from the birds kept in dovecots as a valuable source of food. They were left to forage for themselves.

Interbreeding between several strains and with wild rock doves has produced considerable variation in their plumage. This has increased further this century by interbreeding with lost racing pigeons.

The rock dove has not been recorded at Wisley, being confined in the wild to the NW coast of Scotland and the outlying islands and to the W and SW coasts of Ireland.

Stock Dove

If you spot a "wood pigeon" without white on its wings or on its neck then it's a stock dove. The close similarity means that this is a much under-recorded species and doesn't even get a mention in the Wisley records until 1955. That was a bad time for the stock dove as toxic seed dressings were then widely used in agriculture and seed is their main food. In areas devoted to agriculture the species was nearly wiped out.

Until the early 19th century they were confined to S and SE England but since then the population has spread out over most of England. At Wisley there are not only good feeding areas to attract them but the farm buildings and mature trees provide nesting holes. They will also use squirrels' dreys, large old bird nests and nesting boxes.

Odd birds were recorded on fourteen days of 1986. Only two flocks have been recorded, both on Wisley Airfield, one of 100 birds on 4.11.1973 and then 40 on 19.11.1978. Occasionally they are recorded flying over the RHS Gardens; indeed in 1984 these comprised the only records.

Wood Pigeon

On November 24th 1973 there descended upon the common at Wisley some 10,000 wood pigeons searching for vegetable food during the hard frosts. When flocks like this, or even larger, come down into a farmer's arable it's not difficult to appreciate why they're ranked our most serious bird pest. The following February (16th) another flock of 1,000 arrived. It is food supplies, especially the acreage of certain crops, that is the chief limiting factor in the pigeon numbers. They are also affected by changes in agricultural practice; until recently they survived over winter on clover and weed seeds in the fallow land left after the corn. Nowadays the rising popularity of winter wheat is taking much of that fallow back into use. There is less seed from weeds due to the use of herbicides. The hungry gap is filled by the adaptable wood pigeons transfering their attentions to the newer crop of oil seed rape.

Sufficient food provides for up to three broods a year, in a platform of twigs so flimsy that you can see through it. The early broods are usually sheltered in evergreens while later ones are to be found out in the deciduous canopies. There they fall foul of Magpies and Jays that account for 97% of egg losses. Nevertheless, enough wood pigeons survive for them to be a familiar bird about Wisley throughout the year.

Collared Dove

This was an oriental bird until the 1930s when it began a massive and rapid expansion across Eurasia. With four to six broods a year there was no shortage of them even though they usually only have two eggs at a time. Within twenty years they were well into Europe and in 1955 reached Britain. The first Surrey record was at Carshalton in 1961.

Wisley provides its favourite habitats with open spaces of seeding grasses and other flowers for food, bushes and trees for nesting and poles with overhead wires for roosting and lookout points. In particular they haunt any likely source of grain, from farms to gardens with poultry. Such opportunities for easy pickings are, however, limited so the Collared Doves have not increased to pest proportions here as they have in some districts. Gardeners have to be wary though, especially as Collared Doves associate so freely with man, his homes and his gardens.

Through the village is an obvious place to look for them and out in the fields when there is seed about. The RHS Garden doesn't attract many but they have nested on the edge of it and out on the common. Wherever there's loose grit on the roadside any member of the dove/pigeon family may be spotted collecting pebbles which are used in their digestive systems for helping to break hard seed cases. Then the Collared Dove is usually seen as slim and sleek but when it settles down to roost it can fluff up its feathers until it looks as plump and fat as any of its relatives.

Turtle Dove

Unlike its other relatives
to be spotted around Wisley, the
Turtle Dove is a summer migrant.
It usually arrives during the
second half of April and remains
until late summer although the
last stragglers may not pass through
Surrey until October.

Numbers had been increasing slightly
but have declined again in the last few
years. This is due to climatic changes
in Africa where it overwinters.

Nests are usually lower than
nine feet, and most likely in bushes
of hawthorn or elder, away from
human interference. There, two
or three broods will be raised,
on a platform of twigs, just like
the other doves and pigeons.
Normally only two eggs are laid
per brood, whichever the species,
and the Turtle Dove is no exception
although its eggs are much smaller
than those of its relatives.

Cuckoo

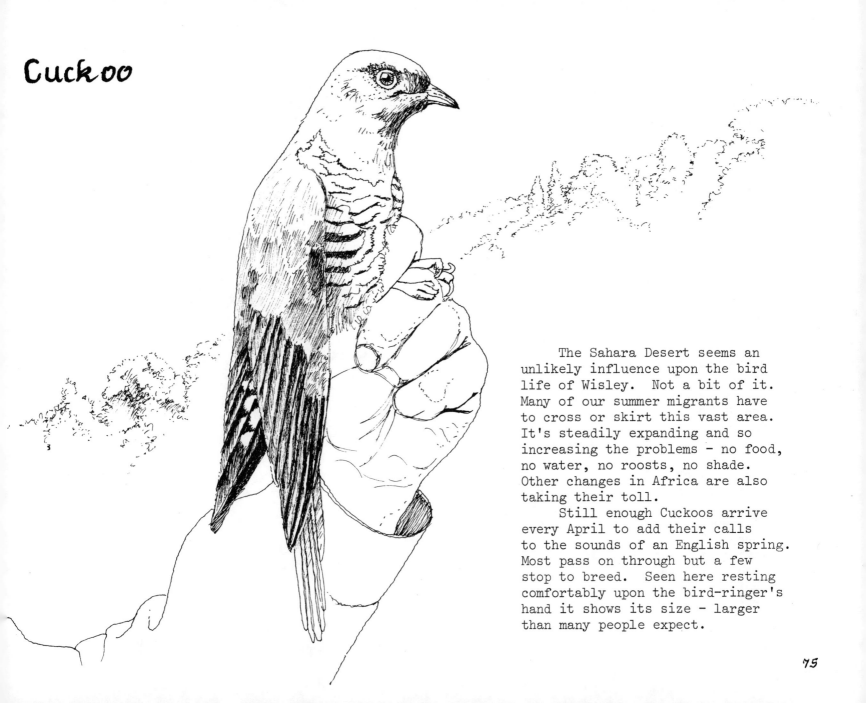

The Sahara Desert seems an unlikely influence upon the bird life of Wisley. Not a bit of it. Many of our summer migrants have to cross or skirt this vast area. It's steadily expanding and so increasing the problems - no food, no water, no roosts, no shade. Other changes in Africa are also taking their toll.

Still enough Cuckoos arrive every April to add their calls to the sounds of an English spring. Most pass on through but a few stop to breed. Seen here resting comfortably upon the bird-ringer's hand it shows its size - larger than many people expect.

75

The cuckoo is an awkward subject for the conservationist. Firstly it prefers a varied habitat of thickets, mature trees and open spaces. Fortunately Wisley is able to offer all these to any Cuckoo that can reach Britain, and looks like being able to continue to do so for quite some time yet. The second great problem arises out of its breeding cycle. The Cuckoo is the only British bird to lay its eggs in other birds' nests and leave the "foster parents" to rear its young. Thus, in terms of conservation, an adequate population of suitable "foster parents" must be maintained as breeding species at Wisley. It is vital that breeding stocks of these species are large enough to withstand the loss of all their young because the infant Cuckoo ejects them out of the nest. As the Cuckoo lays up to 25 eggs these losses are considerable.

Hosts are selected by size and by diet. They must be smaller than a blackbird and must not be a seed-eater for the young Cuckoo is obviously fed on whatever the host would normally feed its own young. This is decided by the Cuckoo laying its eggs in a nest of the same species as had originally raised that Cuckoo. Consequently, continuity of breeding species is important

At Wisley the host is usually the Dunnock except where it is scarce as out on the common. Then a Tree Pipit or a Meadow Pipit is chosen. It is suspected that Robins and Wrens have also been chosen.

Barn Owl

This well-known and useful
bird is unfortunately familiar
from pictures rather than from
real life. It's declining
dramatically and efforts are
being made to conserve it.
It's been given protection under
law but just as important will
be the current programmes to
encourage it to breed.

It's a bird of farms and
fields, nesting in the
traditional farm buildings.
These places are rapidly
disappearing so any reader
living near open fields is
urged to provide a nest box.
Barn Owls take to these
readily and bird conservation
organisations will provide all
the information needed.

At Wisley the Barn Owl
occurs in the records right
back to 1907 but it's a rare
sight today. One was recorded
in 1964. Wisley Farm still
has buildings that ought to
be suitable for breeding but
is not used at present.
Nevertheless, when the farm
was used for filming in 1987
the Barn Owl moved in to roost
in the film set.

Little Owl

This is the easiest owl to
see by day especially as it tends
to perch prominently in view, but
is often missed because people don't
expect an owl to be so small. It's
about 9 inches long, like a song thrush
but plump.

It likes open areas with mature
trees around, in which it can find
suitable nesting holes. Thus the RHS
Garden offer good opportunities for
spotting it. In 1984 one was heard
regularly through October in the trees
around the Garden entrance. They have
nested in the mature oaks by the new
arboretum and also been recorded from
the wild garden and the pinetum.

It is not a
native species but was
introduced in several places
by the Victorians. Those in Surrey are possibly
derived from those released in Kent in 1874-80.
Certainly by 1930 they'd been recorded in every
county south of the Humber, only to suffer
decline with other predators from pesticide
poisoning in the 1950s and 60s. Numbers have
now built up again.

It has few enemies but is sometimes taken
by its larger relative, the Tawny Owl.

Young Tawny Owls.

79

Tawny Owl

All the trees around Wisley ensure that the familiar owl
hoot is regularly heard after dusk, especially from December
to February which is the courting time for Tawny Owls. Large
areas of trees are their preferred habitats.

Hearing owls is one thing, seeing them is another.
Hunting usually takes place during the hours of darkness and
during the day they are notoriously difficult to see. Often
they roost against a tree trunk and then their magnificent
camouflage proves so effective. In winter they often roost
very high and then they're even easier to miss.

In Spetember 1984 one delighted visitors by flying across
the RHS arboretum in broad daylight but that was quite exceptional.

It only breeds in the
years of plentiful
food supplies but once
the eggs have hatched
there is a very high
chance of all the owlets
leaving the nest. Any
intruder, including man,
will be attacked viciously
and driven off. Twice in
recent years very young owls
have been discovered, proving
that they do breed with success
locally. Young owls found "abandoned" should always
be left; they're not nearly as abandoned as we might
think.

The jackdaw boxes in the RHS Gardens have been
adopted by Tawny Owls for roosting and it is hoped
that breeding will follow.

Unfortunately Tawny Owls are still
shot. Others are killed by cars and
this is often the only time that many
people ever see one - in the headlights
or dead on the roadway. Nevertheless,
with the Little Owl, this is the most
frequent owl at Wisley.

Nightjar

The nightjar, so rich in folklore, has unfortunately been declining gradually in Britain over the last century. Wisley was one of its strongholds but since 1981 it has made only brief fleeting visits. In that year there were still five pairs found to be breeding on the common. The building of the M25 and the invasions of birch and pine are no encouragement for it to return. Every effort needs to be made if this bird is to stay on the Wisley list. An essential requirement is bare ground for on this the two eggs are laid. Of these, only one, on average, fledges successfully. That's a very low rate upon which to build a future.

Nightjars arrive by night from Africa during April and May. They then advertise their presence from a song perch with a loud churring noise; so loud it can be heard 2km away on a clear night. Going out to hear this amazing call is one of the highlights of the bird watcher's year. A lesser sound is the way it claps its wings in flight. For these delights it's worth visiting the common from mid-May to August.

Nightjar - open and shut.

Laying begins in the second half of June and the young are soon left in the care of the male while the female lays a second clutch in another scrape. Fledglings from the first brood migrate straight away in July but the main migration is from August to October. During this busy time they can be spotted hunting on the wing, like a small falcon - at dusk. The beak opens wide and broad with a scoop of surrounding whiskers to trap moths and airborne spiders which are its main prey.

Nightjar has to perch along a branch rather than across it because legs so feeble.

Swift

English summer evenings would not be
quite the same without the loud Screeee of the
Swifts. Every season this summer migrant can be
seen high in the skies over Wisley as they hawk for
food. All the insects and airborne spiders that they
need are collected on the wing for they never land on
the ground. If one is forced down it dies because its
legs are too weak and its wings too long for it to be
able to launch itself again. Even the grass, leaves
and feathers used in nest building are snatched from
the winds.

Closer views of the Swift are less
predictable. When the weather keeps insects
low then the Swifts hunt low but at such a
speed that they're still difficult to see in
detail. Occasionally they can be seen in spring
clutching the side of a building as they look for nest sites.
At Wisley they fail to find any to their liking and so this is not
one of the breeding species of the village.

Greatest activity to watch is naturally when there are nestlings
to feed and in a good year this lasts for 35 days or more - much more in
adverse seasons when it can take up to 56 days to find enough food to
bring the nestlings up to full strength for leaving the nest.

Kingfisher

Photographs of the beautiful kingfisher appear so regularly that many people can name it who wouldn't claim to know very much about British Birds. Far fewer have ever seen a live one. This is partly due to many of the photographs taking away a sense of scale and so people look for something far larger than it really is ($7\frac{1}{2}$ ins). The little sketch of one on a ringer's hand may help.

Secondly, the kingfisher flies at such a speed that it's easily missed. The loud "Chee" call is often the first indication that there is one about but that's no help to readers who have not had the chance to learn to recognise it for what it is !

However attractive we may find this bird it is a savage and successful hunter and so the main drawing has been enlarged above life-size to give a view closer to that seen by its smaller prey.

Wisley is a good place to look for kingfishers. Up to three pairs are resident along the river with two of them within the RHS Garden. When the river is in flood and too clouded for them to find fish at all easily, they go off poaching from the Seven Acres Lakes in the RHS Garden, and from the formal pool by the main buildings there. At the latter they use the rescue pole as their vantage point from which to plunge into the water. That's a sight enjoyed by the workers in the laboratory from their windows but outside visitors frighten them off and so few people see this performance.

The sandy banks cut by the river provide good sites for nesting burrows but the banks are fragile and should not be clambered over by over-enthusiastic readers. Sit quietly early in the morning and you're more likely to see one. Activity is usually intense and noisy when the young are about to leave the nest and then there's an even better chance of seeing this beautiful bird.

Green Woodpecker

The laughing call or "yaffle" of this bird can be heard throughout the year at Wisley. There are many mature trees into which nesting holes can be excavated. Tracking down the tapping noise is a good way to locate this rather shy bird. Other birds can make a similar noise so you may be caught out ! It is most often the male Green Woodpecker that makes the nest hole; he has red centres in his black moustaches which are absent in the female.

Green Woodpeckers feed on ants which they collect with their incredible tongues that can be extended by over four inches. Some ants can be collected off the trees but for the main meals the Green Woodpeckers descend to the ground.

Short grassland can be rich in ants but less of the grass nowadays is cropped short enough due to the decline in sheep farming.

Alternatively they will feed on open heathland but with the decline in rabbit grazing this too is

becoming overgrown. The RHS Gardens attract them to the Fruit Fields, the New Arboretum and Howard's Field with the occasional sighting elsewhere.

juvenile Green Woodpecker.

Greater Spotted Woodpecker

Whereas the Green Woodpecker needs open spaces within easy reach of the trees, the Greater Spotted Woodpecker is more strictly a woodland bird, whether it's coniferous or deciduous. It is the commonest of the woodpeckers at Wisley, being recorded almost daily.

It has become tolerant of man and moved into the street and garden trees of suburban areas and can be seen throughout Wisley village. A traditional supply of mature and dead trees are still plentiful at Wisley to provide nesting sites. They also provide food because it does not follow the Green Woodpecker in having a preference for ants but will eat all sorts of wood-boring larvae and other invertebrates. They even take woodlice which many birds reject. Therefore numbers do not decline as severely as the Green Woodpecker's during hard winter weather. It will take seeds then and has adapted to taking peanuts and other food from garden bird tables. These contribute significantly to its survival in any suburban area, where dead and rotting trees are scarce. Peanut holders have been hung in Howard's Field at Wisley to attract them for ringing. Fresh birds are caught each year proving the success of the many occupied nest holes in the RHS Garden, and throughout the wooded parts of the district.

Woodpeckers excavate their own holes each year. Afterwards they are utilised by other species and may be visited again by the Greater Spotted Woodpeckers which are happy to take eggs and chicks to supplement their diet.

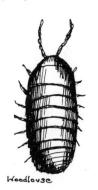

Woodlouse

Lesser Spotted Woodpecker

It's only the size of a sparrow and blends so well into the dappled shadows and patterned bark of the trees that it is rarely seen. This, together with its shyness, makes it a very under-recorded species.

Its preferences are similar to those of the Greater Spotted Woodpecker but do not conflict. They will share habitats but not tolerate overlapping nest sites. The Lesser Spotted Woodpecker drills out holes not less than two inches in diameter, often in the underside of branches. At Wisley they often choose the soft wood of alder trees. There are several groves of these such as along the lane between the church and the canal. Breeding has not been proven in the last five years.

Although breeding is difficult to prove the regular presence of this bird which is normally very sedentary suggests that it is successful at breeding locally. The two caught in the ringers' mist net on March 6th 1984 were thought to have been performing their courtship flight; the male has a very attractive floating display flight but this is rarely seen.

A single bird was spotted again at the end of that month while in 1985 there were three separate sightings in different parts of the area. They occur in the surveys of 1909, 1949 and 1955.

This is one of the birds to benefit from the outbreak of Dutch Elm Disease. The failing trees hosted a rich supply of invertebrate food under the bark but elms are not used for nest holes. Once they were dead the numbers of this Woodpecker declined again.

Skylark

Rising up out of the grasses at the walker's feet is often the best view many people ever get of the Skylark. Its song, however, has been immortalised by poets and writers for all time. There's a strange fascination in watching it rise, almost vertically, into the sky until it disappears from view. At that point it's risen about 1000 ft. Then down it floats, throwing its 'scroobling' song to the ground. All this can be enjoyed at Wisley.

It's a bird of the grasslands, especially short grass. There it hides its well-camouflaged nest under a tussock and always prefers to leave it by creeping away some distance before rising. This makes the nest notoriously difficult to find and with it the proof of breeding. Nevertheless, healthy populations of Skylarks at Wisley throughout the years testifies to their success.

The pasture fields are obvious places to seek them. Indeed the Skylark is one of the birds that has increased with the modern trend towards larger fields. In the RHS Garden look in the Fruit Fields and the New Arboretum.

During winter they can be seen flying around although many people have difficulty in telling one species of flying brown blob from any other. They're easier to identify when on the ground especially if flocked onto arable land during hard times, when up to 96% of their day is spent seeking food. The Wisley fields do not grow lettuce, peas and sugar beet which are the Skylarks' favourites so they are not the pest here that they are in some places.

89

Sand Martin

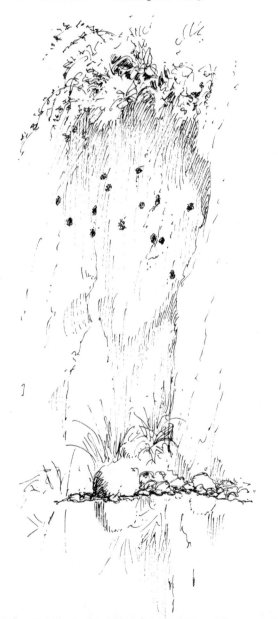

From the third week of March is the time to watch for the return of this summer migrant. It's one of the earliest. Unfortunately it's become a scarce sight in the last three years as its migration route takes it through one of the drought stricken regions of Africa. This is now so extensive that only a small proportion survive to fly on and reach Britain. There had been an earlier population crash in 1974.

Even before that the Sand Martin had ceased to breed at Wisley. They excavate nursery burrows in vertical banks and cliffs, so at Wisley, until ten to fifteen years ago, they utilised the river cuttings. These old sites can still be recognised. They were in use in 1955 and right back in 1909 but now the nearest breeding site is at Papercourt in the adjoining district to the south west.

Although often associated with water they will utilise any earth face that is soft enough for them to tunnel into, even if close to man's activities. From here they will travel several kilometres to seek food. This is caught on the wing. Insects in the airspace over water are harvested intensively and freshly fledged young are taken to reeds etc. by water for the night's roost. Feeding does, however, take place in any airspace and so they can be watched hawking all about Wisley, including over the RHS Garden. Often they are mixed with Swallows and House Martins from which they can be distinguished by being the smallest of the three.

Swallow

A swallow is all feathers. Inside is a tiny body weighing only a couple of ounces and yet able to store enough energy to power it to Britain all the thousands of miles from the Transvaal and S.W.Cape of Africa. Heat and cold, deserts and seas, the powerful forces of migration bring it here every spring, arriving usually by mid-April but occasionally as early as March.

It then risks further hazards by nesting in association with man - under busy road bridges yet aerobatically avoiding high vehicles, under house porches defiant of curious children, in sheds and barns to tantalise cats - returning each year to the same sites and same appreciation from man.

Swallows are in all the Wisley reports since 1907. Until 1985 they nested regularly in the RHS Garden — the most watched site being in the loft over the outbuilding of the Plant Centre. Cats destroyed that in 1984 and the swallows haven't returned since. Previously they also nested in the loft by the Formal Pool, the Glass Dept. shed, the Alpine Dept. garage and even in the Director's garage. Nowadays they've retreated to the farm and stables in the village but can be seen hawking for insects throughout the area. Particularly likely places to spot them are by the sewage works, the river bridge and over the allotments.

House Martin

Originally nesting on the cliffs, as some still do, the House Martin has been moving inland and adopting house walls for hundreds of years now. They were doing so at Wisley in 1909 when there were just a very few houses and most of those were comparatively new. It's a bird that's quick to investigate new potential so it's always worth putting up the nest boxes that have been especially designed for them. Site them with care as the birds drop quite a mess underneath! Contrary to popular belief House Martins are not so very fussy about the direction in which the wall faces as is shown by their nests on the RHS Laboratory and Hostel walls. Boxes should be high enough to benefit from the shadow cast by the eaves.

April is the time to look out for them. They returned on the 12th in 1984 and the 18th in 1985. Soon they can be watched collecting mud for nest building or for repairs; even a shrinking puddle will attract them. Around the farmyard area is a good place to look.

This activity is repeated on a smaller scale later in the summer when a few pairs build a new nest for their second brood. This obviously delays the cycle and some young are still in the nest as late as October. They departed on the 18th in 1984 and on the 16th in 1985.

Good numbers breed around Wisley. House Martins are common and widespread in England generally, on the increase in London, but with the highest densities in the mixed farmland of the lowlands, so Wisley suits them well.

The House Martin was so named by the great naturalist
Gilbert White, in 1767, to distinguish it from
the Sand Martin. White was intrigued to know
whether such birds hibernated in ponds or
migrated. He watched the martins gathering
with Swallows on the Thames osier beds
whereas at Wisley they have to use
overhead wires. Flocks of over
200 can be seen in the autumn
around the village and the
sewage works. Then they're
off to Africa for the
winter - not into
ponds !

Flocks on overhead wires
in autumn are often a
mixture of House Martins and
Swallows. Even when starkly
silhouetted they can be distinguished
by their tails; the notched ones
belong to House Martins while the deeply
forked ones belong to Swallows. As they
move about this shows.

95

The Pipits

    Pipits are among those awkward little brown birds that so many
beginners find confusing. The Tree Pipit can be distinguished from
the Meadow Pipit by its slightly brighter colouring and different
song but only of course if the observer is already familiar with the
Meadow Pipit ! That can be achieved through the winter when the Tree
Pipit is out of the country. The illustration is of a Meadow Pipit.

Tree Pipit

The migrant Tree Pipit arrives from early April and seeks open areas with fence posts or similar distinct perches from which to sing. From these it flies up high and then parachutes down in full chorus to alight on the same 'song post' or another one nearby. This behaviour is typical whereas the Meadow Pipit parachutes right down to the ground with its song.

Listen for the Tree Pipit's song from mid-April until July.

Meadow Pipit

The Meadow Pipit can be distinguished from the Tree Pipit when in song flight for it descends to the ground rather than to a 'song perch'.

It's resident at Wisley throughout the year but in severe winter weather may move south, even as far as France or Spain. Then it is replaced by birds from further north or from the Continent.

Like the Tree Pipit it prefers open countryside, like the common. In addition look for it around the sewage works and in the farm fields, especially when livestock are present.

The Meadow Pipit has been logged at Wisley in all the bird reports, except the first, in 1909.

It feeds and nests in open ground including freshly felled woodland. It will also use newly set plantations but only until the herbage grows tall.

The Tree Pipit occurs in all the Wisley bird reports since 1907. In that year it nested in the rubbish yard of the RHS Garden. In 1987 one sang for a mate by the Plant Centre but moved on. Two or three pairs have used the common regularly in recent years and that's the best place to seek them.

Yellow Wagtail

Another bird that over-winters in Africa is the Yellow Wagtail which leaves for its northern breeding grounds earlier than the Swallows and Martins. It arrives back in England from mid-March onwards and as it passes Wisley in those few weeks, it offers the best chances of being spotted. When they pass again, on their return journey in September/October is another good time to seek them. This happens every year but so quickly that in some years they miss being recorded.

It likes wet meadows, marshy places and sewage works, all of which Wisley has to offer, so it is possible that some may stay to breed but this has not yet been proven.

Grey Wagtail

The Grey Wagtail does not migrate so it chooses its habitat according to the food supply It is a water-side bird whether by fast flowing streams or sluggish canals and even the over-flow systems from lakes and reservoirs. During severe winters when food is scarce and water freezes over they tend to move to the warmer south and west of England. During hard spells they have even been known to take bread put out for garden birds.

Grey Wagtails have been recorded at Wisley in all the old reports and are usually present throughout the year. There are plenty of wet places to suit them, not just by the rivers and the water meadows but all about the R.H.S. Garden and they even visit the little ponds in the village gardens.

The most likely place to be sure of spotting them is from the river bridge by the sewage works.

Unlike the Yellow Wagtail the Grey will live with other birds and congregate with Pied Wagtails. Both will roost in groups of up to 50 birds in buildings, reed beds and brambles.

Pied Wagtail

Skittering around garden lawns, this is a familiar and much loved species, earning local nicknames which in Surrey include Willy Wagtail and Tritty Wagtail. More officially, it has been known as the Water Wagtail but nowadays this is misleading, as it has spread out into a whole variety of habitats from farms to cities but not yet in woodland or bare mountains.

At Wisley they are a familiar sight throughout the R.H.S. Garden for they accept the presence of so many people and readily nest within their close proximity. Some of the more interesting examples from the records include:-

1906 - 1st May, nesting inside the garden frames and in the flower pots;

1947 - were breeding annually and for several years a pair had hidden their nest in a tea rose climbing on the laboratory wall;

1983 - a pair was found nesting in a pile of rocks near the glasshouses. The nestlings were ringed and all successfully fledged;

1984 - a pair nested in a stack of lights by
&   the glasshouses and another pair moved
1985   inside the Red Delphiniums' Glasshouse to nest in a flower pot. Yet another pair had put the laboratory wall back into use and again the following year.
In 1985 the glasshouse pair chose an inside site again. This time it was the heating control box suspended in one of the glasshouses but the young abandoned the nest when an over-enthusiastic film crew became too intrusive. Nevertheless, they all survived. (Basis of the illustration)
Nests are surprisingly difficult to find even when the adults can be seen returning with beaks full of food for the nestlings.
Elsewhere at Wisley the Pied Wagtail can be seen about all grassland sites, from the pasture fields to the lawns in village gardens where they dash around, snapping up insects and are a familiar daily sight. They can also be seen outside the gardens hunting along the roadways. Large numbers collect at the sewage works which is obviously a good place for flies and other insects.

Juvenile Pied
Wagtails.

101

Wren

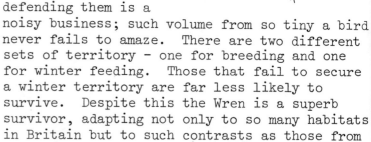

Troglodytes troglodytes is the scientific name of the Wren, taken from the mythical cave dwellers, because the bird builds a domed cave-like nest. In fact the male builds a whole series and then conducts his mate on a tour of inspection. She has the last word and the one she chooses is the one he will line warmly with hair and feathers. He leaves just enough space for her inside but as the family grows so the loosely but carefully woven nest expands with them. There may be six or eight youngsters but as many as sixteen have been recorded.

Intense cold spells decimate the Wren populations. Their tiny bodies conserve too little heat and what they can generate from scant winter food is used up in getting it. One way of reducing heat loss is to roost communally, all packed together in a dry windproof place such as in a nest box. Fifty in a single box is on record. After heavy losses in severe winters numbers are soon recouped as Wrens have two or three of their large broods every season.

The Wren is therefore easy to see because it's always active; food for the family all summer, food for itself all winter; a never-ending struggle.

It is soon heard too. Territories are essential for its survival and defending them is a noisy business; such volume from so tiny a bird never fails to amaze. There are two different sets of territory - one for breeding and one for winter feeding. Those that fail to secure a winter territory are far less likely to survive. Despite this the Wren is a superb survivor, adapting not only to so many habitats in Britain but to such contrasts as those from Japan round to Morocco and up to Iceland (the Vikings called it "rindill" meaning "little tail" which we have by now shortened to Wren. We still use the diminutive names too, as in Jenny Wren or, in Surrey, Juggy or Puggy Wren.

In 1906 it was recorded as common at Wisley and it still is. Look everywhere that provides cover. Of the more interesting records there was a pair in 1984 that moved into a RHS Glasshouse to nest among Fuchsias in a hanging basket while others were concealing their nests in compost heaps in the Wild Garden and the RHS Plant Centre. Another pair tried to take over a House Martins' nest under the laboratory eaves but House Sparrows evicted them.

Tomb sculpture ~ Wotton Churchyard, Surrey.

103

Dunnock

The Dunnock occurs in the Wisley records (since 1906) as the Hedge Sparrow, in the books of last century as the Hedge Accentor and in Surrey dialect as the Shuffle Bird. As soon as it begins to rain they shuffle out from low cover to feed at the edge of open spaces.

The male doesn't have strikingly different plumage with which to attract the female and so it is she who does most of the displaying. She droops and quivers her wings and turns to wave her behind at him as recorded in the three little sketches reproduced here from a sketchbook. He rushes in to try and peck her behind as a preliminary to mating, if she will let him. However, she doesn't always submit. She may move off and they'll chase each other around some more in a weird little dance.

The scene becomes even more interesting if a third bird arrives. That'll be another male, for this species regularly associates in threes as well as the more usual pairs. The new arrival is most likely to be driven off by the first male but may be tolerated by him if he shows submission by drooping his wings. He'll take advantage of the female if he gets the chance and indeed she will often encourage him. That's to her advantage because if he successfully mates with her then he'll help feed the subsequent nestlings. He will have nothing to do with them if they are the progeny of the other male, even though the trio have stayed together.

Logically this suggests there are more males than females. This is probably so because during hard weather the stronger birds (usually male) drive weaker birds (usually female) away from sources of food and thus they are more likely to die. Thus defence of the winter feeding territories provides yet another range of displays, further complicated at nesting time when the males and females have separate feeding territories. There's plenty for the bird watcher to enjoy although the Dunnock is a shy bird, best watched from house or car windows.

Dunnocks occur throughout the Wisley area. See also Cuckoo entry.

Robin

The Robin needs no introduction and it's just as familiar around the gardens and shrubby places at Wisley as it is everywhere else, and according to the records it always has been. The only essential is for there to be low cover, preferably with trees. Deep in this cover is the natural place for them to hide their nests and very well hidden they are too.

This is the little bird that earns so much affection and then shocks its admirers for being so vicious in the defence of its territory. Workers at the RHS Garden entered the Plant Centre Glasshouse one day to find a Robin hacking at an opponent which it had successfully pinned on its back on the ground. Its a regular occurrence for a Robin to adopt a glasshouse when the weather is severe. The males defend one territory for the whole of their lives; the females have to overwinter away from the breeding territory (up to 5km) and thus come to gardens seeking food. They're fond of fruit in the winter, otherwise they prey upon invertebrates. Many become very tame. Visitors to the RHS Garden have found that the Robin with the Rock Garden in its territory would feed from the hand.

Nesting in close proximity to man, often in unexpected places, is another well-known habit. Once, an empty cement bag was left by the Information Centre long enough to become half covered with leaves and then staff noticed food being taken inside. Lifting the torn edge they peeped in to find five youngsters in a nest. These were left and successfully fledged.

Fledgeling Robin still with its thrush-like speckles.

Nightingale

The Nightingale, famed for its song, is a difficult species to spot. It likes areas with thick ground cover and then all you're likely to see is a brown shape moving through the stems and thorns. Attention is likely to be drawn to it by a burst of distinctive song. Every now and again one will perch more openly and sing more fully. It will do this at any time of the day but will also do so after dark. The first and last hours of the night are its favourite times for doing this.

Wisley does not provide enough of the thick ground cover preferred by this species. In 1907 they were recorded nesting low down in Rhododendrons. By 1947, referring to Battleston Hill in the RHS Garden, it was recorded that they "used to sing hereabouts but not now." No further mention of them occurs until the 1962 Surrey Bird Report, which records nesting between the neighbouring districts of Ripley and Ockham. Another silence follows until 1984 when singing was recorded from Wisley Village and from the RHS Garden between 6th May and 3rd June. In 1985 singing was heard on just one night, 19th April.

Nightingales are summer migrants and must pass through on passage so there is always the possibility of recording one. Even in favoured haunts their numbers are declining.

Blackbird

With a gold ring around its shiny eyes and a gold bill, all set off against the black plumage, a cock Blackbird looks quite exotic. It chooses some quite exotic nest sites too. The large greenhouse in the RHS Garden is used annually and once they used a very spiney inhabitant of the Cactus House.

Through all the records the Blackbird has been plentiful around Wisley, in the full range of habitats.

Memorable encounters are usually at nesting time. The Plant Centre staff had to dissuade a customer from buying a potted conifer when they found a blackbird sitting on eggs inside it. Another member of staff had an old London taxi parked behind the shop for two or three days - long enough for a Blackbird to nest under the bonnet and be sitting on eggs.

As soon as the summer's fruit begins
to redden it attracts the Blackbirds. Any
strawberry beds become a prime target but
better views of the Blackbird feeding can
be had a little later when they move up
into the berried trees, such as rowans,
to strip them in full view. Many of the
village gardeners have planted ornamental
berried trees so this is a worthwhile
place to look aswell as in the RHS Garden.

Later still, cold weather lures them
away from their usual territories to
congregate around fruit trees to feast
upon windfalls on the ground and upon any
fruit left on the branches. At these
times the RHS Fruit Fields are the most
rewarding places to sit and watch.

Other members of the thrush family,
such as Fieldfares and Redwings, will
join them and add considerable variety and
interest to a little while spent watching.
These thrushes are well known as winter
migrants but what is less well known is
the huge influx of Blackbirds that arrives
in this country from north east Europe
whenever the winter hardens.

Fledgelings
seem all beak
and legs at first
as in these sketches.
They leave the nest
without tail feathers
so early flights are
very unbalanced, with abrupt
landings, making them easy prey
for cats, stoats, foxes, etc.
Children should be encouraged not
to rescue them but to leave them to
the adult birds to guide
them to safety. The young
Blackbird (top right) was
much more advanced and had gorged itself fully on
the rowan berries. Less contented was the adult
cock (top left) which flew into the bush so aggressively
in defending its breeding territory that it overbalanced
forwards and fell with a flurry into the brambles.

Fieldfare

When autumn wears on and birds gather in the bare hedgerows
seeking the last of the berries then it's worth seeing if
any are Fieldfares. They are primarily winter visitors
to Britain, arriving from Scandinavia as soon as they've
stripped the rowan berries there. That means the
first arrive in September followed by the main influx
during October and November. The size of our own
berry harvest and the earliness or lateness of our
winter determines how quickly these birds move
south. At Wisley it's worth looking out for them
from mid-October onwards.

To the experienced ear it's their loud and distinctive chucking call that draws the eye
upward as they pass over. They are often just as noisy when feeding and that's usually out in
the open. It's a communal activity but with aggressive behaviour in defending a good food supply.

Fruit and insects comprise their normal diet with apples, including rotten ones, a very
firm favourite. The RHS Orchards attract flocks of two to three hundred when the cold increases
so this is by far the best place to see them at close quarters as they move noisily among the
apple trees or feast upon the dumps of gathered windfalls. They may feed with other thrushes
(and Starlings) but their silver grey backs and black tails make them easily distinguished.

They are not able to withstand the cold as successfully as Blackbirds. Maybe this is due to
food shortages which Blackbirds overcome by frequenting gardens to take food provided by man. In
1985 a number of Fieldfares were ringed at Wisley in January and weighed. A month later, a very
cold month, some were caught and weighed again. Minimum weight had dropped from 110 g to 86 g.
Maximum weight had dropped from 128 g to 101 g. The thaw arrived a couple of days later,
softening the apples again and enabling the Fieldfares to regain their strength. No dead
Fieldfares were recorded.

Apart from the RHS Orchard they frequent the palatable berried trees and shrubs in the RHS
Garden and the village gardens and along the hedgerows so there are plenty of places to see them.
It's usually the beginning of April when the last Fieldfares leave on the return journey north.
The fruit has been stripped by now so they turn to a diet of invertebrates - a good source of
protein ready for the rigours of breeding. At this time they feed out in the pastures.

Song Thrush

Killed by a passing car, this casualty gives a good opportunity to draw attention to the dangers of passing traffic to any low-flying bird. Owls seem to suffer most because they get dazzled by the car headlights at night before being struck. Insects get killed or stunned in high numbers so the roadsides become good hunting grounds. Most noticeable here are the scavengers, such as members of the crow family, which not only benefit from the luckless Song Thrushes but all manner of squashed creatures from hedgehogs to lizards basking on the hot surface.

Song Thrushes hunt along the road edges for worms that have crawled out onto the surface or which are trying to avoid drowning in surface water after rain. If the thrushes aren't quick they are in danger of being run over.

Worms are a favourite food so around Wisley it's worth checking any areas of short grass where the Song Thrushes can spot worms more easily. They share the family's liking for fruit and join their relatives in the RHS Orchard all the time there is fruit available. Other rewarding places to seek them are the RHS Pinetum and the Riverside Walk. In cold winter weather when the ground is too frozen for them to be able to get at the worms they move off to milder districts. They're replaced by Scandinavian birds moving south on the same venture. Very few of these actually overwinter here.

The Song Thrush doesn't do very well at Wisley. They seem to suffer from predation, mainly from the ever increasing numbers of Magpies. These relish eggs and those of the Song Thrush are easy to find. The nests are not especially well concealed, being lodged in a forked branch usually less than six feet from the ground of any tree or bush. Magpies search their way through such sites, diligently seeking nests. The large open cup of the Song Thrush's nest, cannot be easy to miss, neither can the eggs. They don't have enough black spots to camouflage their pale (sky blue to us) base colour.

Song Thrushes can often be located by sound. As their name suggests, they sing distinctively. Very often this is from a regular "song post" in some prominent position where the male can be well seen by the female he's trying to attract, or by invaders of his territory.

A second sound is a knocking as a thrush smashes the shell off a snail on a chosen "anvil" before eating them. Snails are an important item in their diet and the same stones acting as anvils are used time and time again; easily identified by the encircling broken shells.

Redwing

114

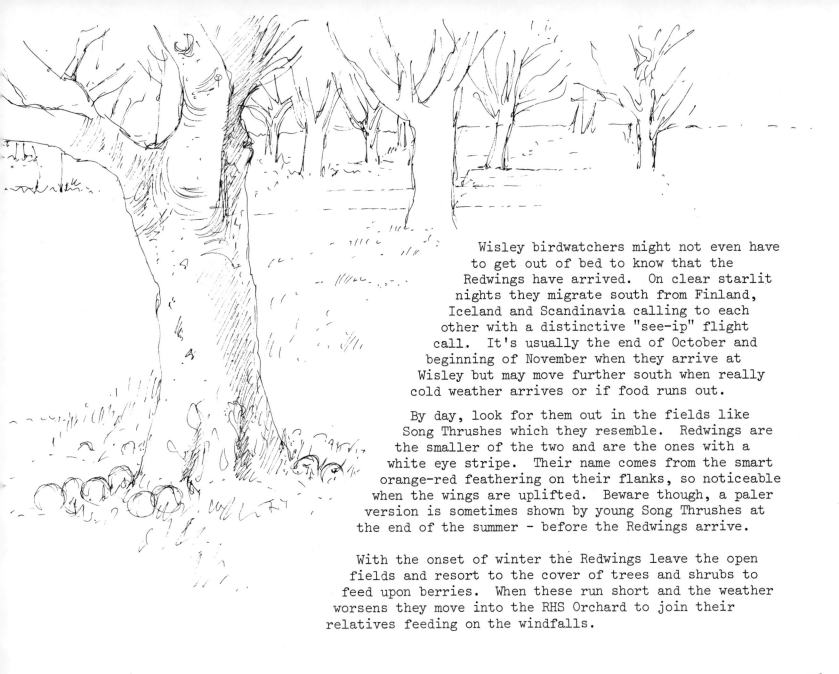

Wisley birdwatchers might not even have to get out of bed to know that the Redwings have arrived. On clear starlit nights they migrate south from Finland, Iceland and Scandinavia calling to each other with a distinctive "see-ip" flight call. It's usually the end of October and beginning of November when they arrive at Wisley but may move further south when really cold weather arrives or if food runs out.

By day, look for them out in the fields like Song Thrushes which they resemble. Redwings are the smaller of the two and are the ones with a white eye stripe. Their name comes from the smart orange-red feathering on their flanks, so noticeable when the wings are uplifted. Beware though, a paler version is sometimes shown by young Song Thrushes at the end of the summer - before the Redwings arrive.

With the onset of winter the Redwings leave the open fields and resort to the cover of trees and shrubs to feed upon berries. When these run short and the weather worsens they move into the RHS Orchard to join their relatives feeding on the windfalls.

Mistle Thrush

The name comes from
the bird's liking for the
berries of Mistletoe but
around Wisley it has to accept
second best, the berries of Holly
and Yew and there aren't many of
the latter either. A well-berried
bush is liable to be guarded against
rival birds. This provides some good
aggressive displays to look out for.

In winter the numbers may be swollen
by migrations from the Continent. British
birds only seem to migrate in their first
winter. In common with so many other British
birds, the northern populations tend to move south
in the winter. In very cold weather look for them in
the flocks of its other thrush relatives in the RHS Orchard etc.

119

Two centuries ago the Mistle Thrush was a bird of wild
and open moorland but gradually it's learnt to accept man
and to move closer to exploit his artificially short grasslands.
Playing fields are much to its liking as a feeding ground and
so are lawns, so the RHS Garden suits it well.

The change of lifestyle has also brought it into a closer
relationship with trees. It's from high in these that it sings
so distinctively and it's up there that it now nests. As with
the Blackbird, breeding begins as early as February in a mild year
and it goes on to raise two or three broods. It's not as plentiful
as it might be though, due to predators raiding the nests.
Woodland opportunists like the Jay and Magpie take eggs
and young nestlings. Just as predatory are the Grey
Squirrels that have spread throughout the Wisley area
this century. The account usually given is that early
broods are more successful at fledging; that later
broods are more often lost to predators striving to
find enough food during their own breeding seasons.
Observations at Wisley suggest that the reverse is true,
for this district at least. Early nests are more easily
found by man and predators because the trees have not yet
unfurled their leaves with which to hide them. The flaw
in this argument is that if the nests are easily found
then of course they are more likely to be robbed.
What is certain is that enough nests are successfully
hidden to maintain the Mistle Thrush as a common bird at
Wisley.

Squirrel
Jay and
Magpie ~
threats to the Mistle Thrush

The Whitethroats

Both these warblers
arrived in the ringers' net
on the same occasion so it was
possible to bring them together
for comparison. They were quickly
photographed for to hold them long
enough to draw from life would have
caused unnecessary stress.

Although this book is not intended as a guide to correct
identification it might be useful to give guidance here
as these two species are often confused by beginners.
In fact the species are quite distinct; it's trying
to remember what goes with which that confuses!

The Lesser Whitethroat has distinctive dark ear coverts, unlike
any other warbler. The Whitethroat has rufus wings and again
this characteristic is not shared by other warblers. Close
inspection in good light shows that the Lesser Whitethroat
has blue grey legs while the Whitethroat has pale brown
legs. The Lesser is smaller by such a tiny amount
that size is no help.

Lesser Whitethroat

This is a secretive little bird arriving in the second half of April. It's travelled all the way from its wintering grounds in Central and West Africa but instead of taking the direct route across the Straits of Gibraltar. it skirts all the way round the eastern side of the Mediterranean.

On arrival the male seeks out tall trees from which to sing for a mate prior to pairing. Once you're familiar with the song this is the easiest way of locating them. Otherwise it means very patiently watching tall hedgerows and thick undergrowth where they choose to live and nest. Fortunately these are still available at Wisley. Bramble patches on the common also attract them as do overgrown gardens and even young conifer plantations.

At Wisley they were recorded breeding in the reed beds by the river back in 1906. By 1949, when a complete list of Wisley birds was compiled, they had gone and were not mentioned at all. They were back on the 1955 list and in recent years have been breeding on the common and in the New Arboretum hedgerows adjacent to the river.

120

121

Whitethroat

     Unlike the Lesser Whitethroat this bird does take the
direct route to Britain from West Africa via the Straits
of Gibraltar. It arrives in mid-April and seeks out thick
scrub whether on the common or in hedgerows. It can
also be found around woodland edges and in the
clearings, wherever there is enough light to
promote the thick ground cover that it likes.
     The Whitethroat also sings for a mate
from a prominent perch but unlike the
Lesser Whitethroat it will sing in
flight. As there are two broods in
a year the males can be heard in
song flight throughout the
breeding season.

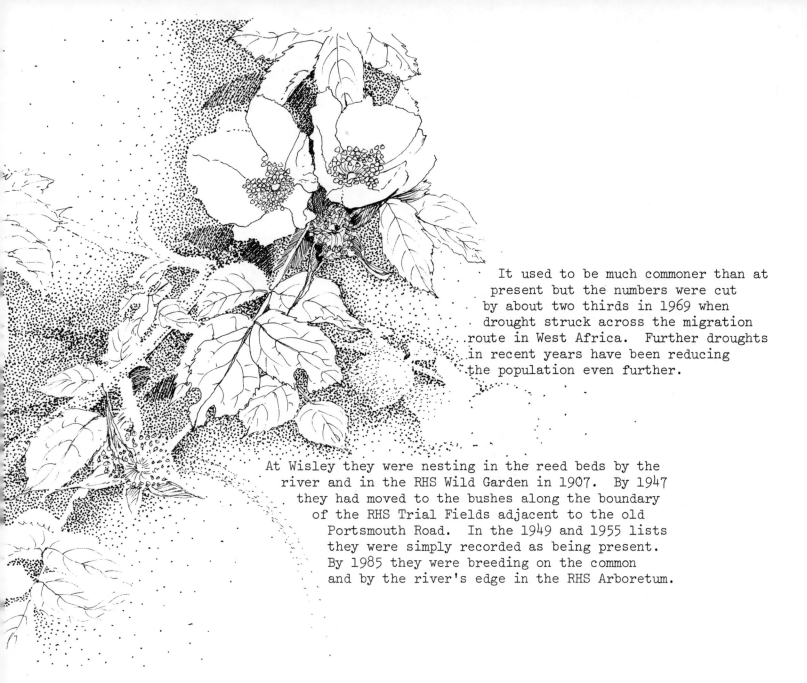

It used to be much commoner than at
present but the numbers were cut
by about two thirds in 1969 when
drought struck across the migration
route in West Africa. Further droughts
in recent years have been reducing
the population even further.

At Wisley they were nesting in the reed beds by the
river and in the RHS Wild Garden in 1907. By 1947
they had moved to the bushes along the boundary
of the RHS Trial Fields adjacent to the old
Portsmouth Road. In the 1949 and 1955 lists
they were simply recorded as being present.
By 1985 they were breeding on the common
and by the river's edge in the RHS Arboretum.

123

Garden Warbler

Garden Warblers prefer open
scrub away from mature woodland,
unlike the Blackcap, and so the two
species do not compete for nesting
sites. Of the two habitats there is
less of the open scrub at Wisley
and so fewer Garden Warblers than
Blackcaps. The two species are often
difficult to see and recognition may
have to rely upon sound. Their song,
however, is notoriously difficult for
some people to distinguish which may
explain why the Garden Warbler was
not listed at all in 1909 nor in
1947. It does occur on the 1949 and
1955 lists but to date the records are
very poor for this species. This may
say more about the bird watchers than
it does about the bird.

Bramble thickets are their chief
nesting site and in recent years they've
used the ones on the river bank by the
Pump House and those in wild corners of
the village. Some of the latter have now
been "tidied up" with the loss of the site.
They are left on the common and also on
the river side of the RHS New Arboretum
in which two pairs nested
in 1985.

Very rarely does the Garden Warbler
overwinter here so look out for it when the
summer migrations arrive in late April. Rather
than looking for this skulking bird, it's often better
to listen for it as the males sing for their mates during
the first couple of weeks after arrival. Having paired, there's
a decline in the singing although it may be heard sporadically
throughout the breeding season. As that begins so late there's
usually only time for one brood. Some pairs manage two.

Warbler country - rough grass, scrub, trees, woodland edges.

125

Blackcap

This can be a tricky one! For one thing it is easy to confuse with a Garden Warbler and for another it is often described as a summer migrant whereas some overwinter in Britain. Fortunately the male's black cap (rich brown in the female) makes it easy to recognise. In winter the only other small birds with a black cap with which a beginner might confuse it are the Willow Tit and the Marsh Tit.

Those that migrate here are among the earliest to arrive, reaching Wisley from the end of March onwards. Very soon they are incubating the first clutch of eggs in a nest less than a metre from the ground. Stray too close and the birds become very vocal with their sharp "tack" alarm calls. Despite this signal the nest is still notoriously difficult to find. One was spotted concealed very cleverly just under a few leaves on the surface of a low bramble bush but by the time the young hatched the canopy was thick with foliage and the nest inaccessible except by the adults approaching it secretly from behind.

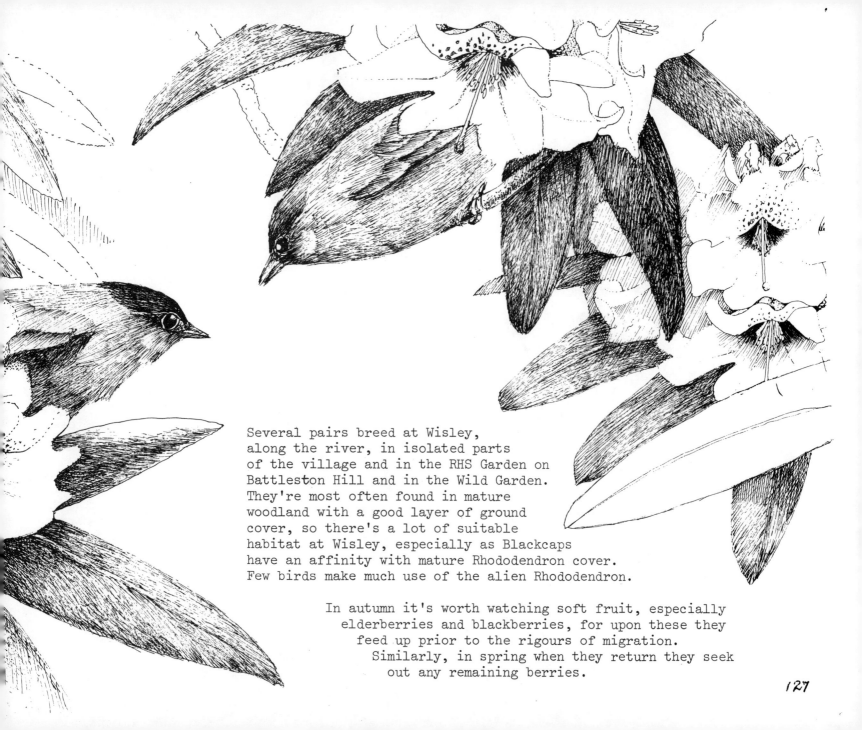

Several pairs breed at Wisley,
along the river, in isolated parts
of the village and in the RHS Garden on
Battleston Hill and in the Wild Garden.
They're most often found in mature
woodland with a good layer of ground
cover, so there's a lot of suitable
habitat at Wisley, especially as Blackcaps
have an affinity with mature Rhododendron cover.
Few birds make much use of the alien Rhododendron.

In autumn it's worth watching soft fruit, especially
elderberries and blackberries, for upon these they
feed up prior to the rigours of migration.
Similarly, in spring when they return they seek
out any remaining berries.

127

Chiffchaff

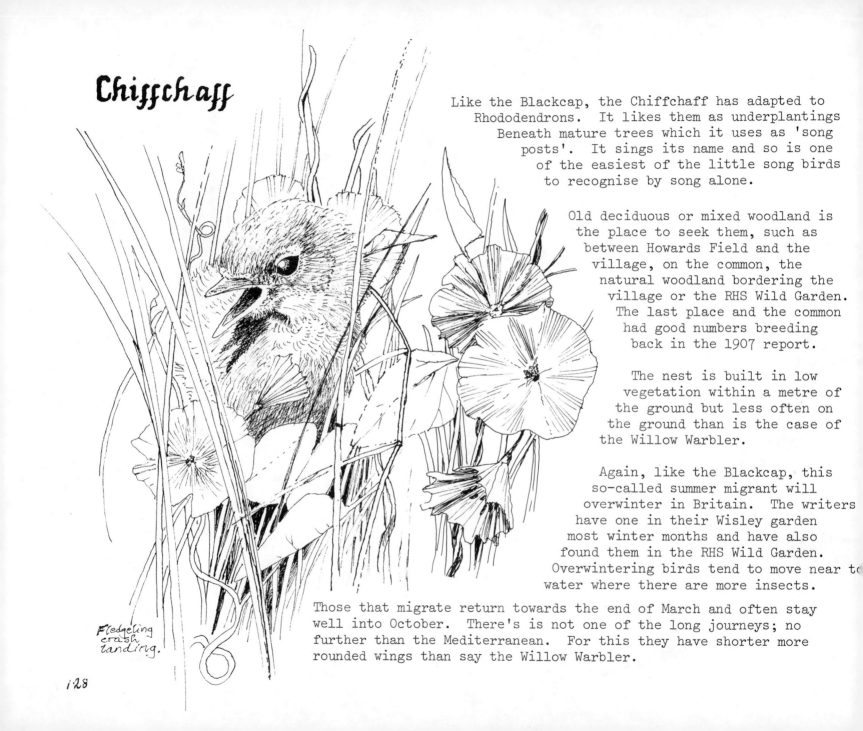

Like the Blackcap, the Chiffchaff has adapted to Rhododendrons. It likes them as underplantings Beneath mature trees which it uses as 'song posts'. It sings its name and so is one of the easiest of the little song birds to recognise by song alone.

Old deciduous or mixed woodland is the place to seek them, such as between Howards Field and the village, on the common, the natural woodland bordering the village or the RHS Wild Garden. The last place and the common had good numbers breeding back in the 1907 report.

The nest is built in low vegetation within a metre of the ground but less often on the ground than is the case of the Willow Warbler.

Again, like the Blackcap, this so-called summer migrant will overwinter in Britain. The writers have one in their Wisley garden most winter months and have also found them in the RHS Wild Garden. Overwintering birds tend to move near to water where there are more insects.

Those that migrate return towards the end of March and often stay well into October. There's is not one of the long journeys; no further than the Mediterranean. For this they have shorter more rounded wings than say the Willow Warbler.

Fledgeling crash landing.

Willow Warbler

Come early April and all around Wisley can be heard the song of the Willow Warbler or the Hawk's Eye as it used to be called in Surrey. The song is a beautiful trill of descending notes and is the clearest way to try and distinguish it from the Chiffchaff that it so closely resembles. Sharp eyes might notice it's slightly more colourful but with paler legs. The wings are longer for covering its greater migration route.

Listen out for it in the RHS Garden, out on the common or around the village, especially in the vicinity of the allotments. In common with other warblers to be found at Wisley it likes the scrubby areas. As nesting sites they must have good ground cover for the Willow Warbler hides its nest on or very close to the ground, tucked away in thick grass tussocks. Don't look where the overhead trees shade out such undergrowth but if enough light can penetrate clearings and rides to promote the grass then the Willow Warbler moves in too.

They're busy birds, with the first clutch of eggs laid during early May, promptly followed by a second, in time for the birds to migrate south from mid to late September.

Proving that breeding has occurred is difficult. There were records for 1947 when the Willow Warblers were frequenting the common and the river bank from the pump house to the village.

Today they are the commonest of the Warblers at Wisley.

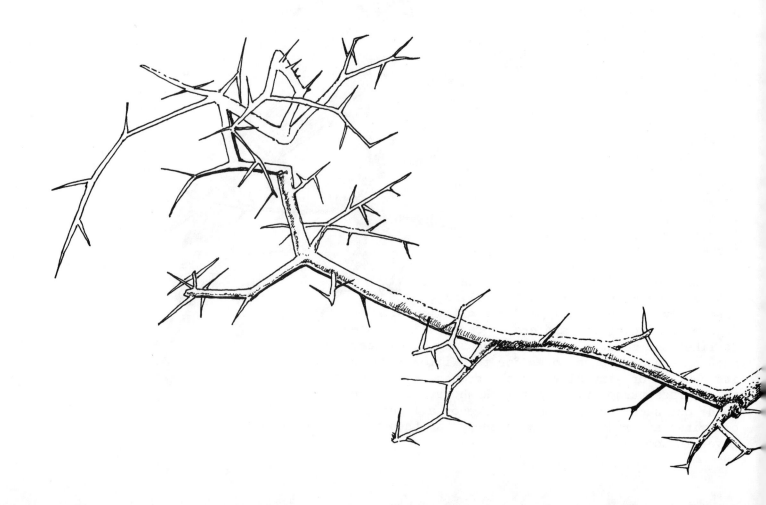

131

Goldcrest

Conifers receive much adverse criticism but there can be words in their favour when it comes to the tiny Goldcrest. Conifers provide their most favoured habitat. Among the dense evergreen foliage they hide from predators, hunt for their food, raise their young and shelter from the cold. Only when the populations get too high do the Goldcrests spill over into other woodland.

Well known for being the smallest British bird (9cm) they are less well known in the field. They can be very difficult to spot in the conifers but once found, and if intent upon feeding in low branches, will often allow someone to approach within a few feet. Active Goldcrests keep up regular calls to each other which can be the best way of locating them. It's a persistent zee-zee-zee (or BBC to some people). However, it's on such a high pitch that it is said that bird watchers know when they are getting old because they can no longer hear a Goldcrest !

Populations are controlled by the weather. Goldcrests are too tiny to store enough energy to get them through prolonged periods of severe frost. The series of hard winters in the mid 1980s has taken its toll. A new strategy for beating the winter is their gradual acceptance of food from bird tables in the village gardens. Maybe they've been introduced to these by the tits with which they often associate. Away from the village gardens it's more usually the Siskins and Coal Tits with which they associate. The most dependable place to find them is in the RHS Pinetum.

The nest is a little hammock slung under a conifer branch and exceptionally difficult to find. Breeding records are therefore scarce. The best indications of breeding success are the parties of newly fledged youngsters which can be located by all the calling.

As winter approaches and the weather worsens so there are influxes of Goldcrests from northern Europe. They may be tiny but they can still cross the sea. Other species making the same journey tend to move south and westwards upon arrival but the Goldcrest shows a tendency to move to the south and east.

A particularly interesting record for the RHS Garden comes from 1947 when evidently "scores" of Goldcrests formed an "annual autumn occurrence" in the wind belt beside the Wild Garden.

These sketches of Goldcrests are reproduced a little larger than life size. They were made when the weather encouraged them to flatten their feathers but in colder times they fluff them out and change their shape into a much more rounded blob-like appearance, just as the Robin is shown on Christmas cards but can be so sleek in the summer.

Spotted Flycatcher

Spotted Flycatchers are often noticed by their distinctive habit of flitting out from a perch to seize an insect in mid air and then returning to the same perch.

They are one of the last of the summer migrants to arrive. The first filter through from mid April, with the main influx by the beginning of May. Look for them along the edges of woodland such as the RHS Wild Garden. If there is water nearby, to increase the numbers of insects, so much the better.

They also associate closely with man, moving into orchards, public parks and gardens, even to the extent of nesting against house walls. Such sites don't have to be quiet either. One pair in 1983 nested in a coconut hanging from a pergola in a Wisley garden. It was within a metre of the back door, used regularly by the family which included children and a dog. They will adopt nest boxes if they are of the open-fronted design.

Nests are built in thick concealing vegetation,
often against a vertical surface or within an
opening in it. Old nests of other species, such
as the Song Thrush and the Swallow, are sometimes
used as a base upon which to build their own new
one.

   It's a neat structure, taking the first clutch of
eggs by the end of May or early in June. Most pairs are
double brooded.

         The nests are so well hidden that confirmation
of breeding often has to wait until the young have fledged.
Then the family groups attract attention with all the noise
they make.

   Over the years the population has been reasonably
stable but there was a sharp decline in 1987.
Prior to that, seven or eight pairs nested
in various parts of the RHS Garden. The
climbers on the laboratory wall have been
a favourite site for many years. The
Walled Garden usually attracts a pair
but although they keep trying the nest
is predated in most years, either by
rodents or by the magpies that nest in
the conifers overlooking the
Walled Garden. There is irony
in those conifers being in a
part of the Garden known as
"The Graveyard".

135

Long-tailed Tit

The Long-tailed Tit has delighted generations of people, so much so that many regions of the country have their own special name for it. In Surrey it was known as the Long Pod.

Unlike the other tits that follow in this book, the Long-tailed Tit builds a nest out in the open, rather than in a hole. It's a famous nest too, for being sculpted out of mosses and lichens into a dome and then lined with hairs and hundreds of feathers, (over 2,000 have been found in some nests). Such a masterpiece takes three weeks to build; it's a wonder that the feathers alone do not take longer to collect.

For safety, nests are wedged deep in a thorn bush or high in the fork of a tree, up to 20 metres from the ground. Nevertheless early nests are often predated because building begins in March when there aren't enough leaves to hide them. Consequently the success rate is only about 33% of nests built.

Inside, 10-12 eggs are usually laid so numbers are still maintained. As this huge family grows so the nest has to stretch; the cobwebs keep it together.

After fledging, the family group stays together, for these are communal birds. Contact is maintained by persistent calling, producing the much-loved "tinkling" music that heralds the approach of a party of Long-tails. They acrobat their way through the twigs searching for food, sometimes low in an old thick hedge or high in the birches on the common. They're very active in their hunting, using their tails to keep their balance, and the whole party quickly passes. Usually bird watchers can keep apace with them. That's easier in the winter when regular watching teaches the extent of the feeding territory. The fun starts when one party strays into the territory of the next and gets caught. Then there's a lot of noise and flitting about by the defending party.

136

The social structure of any party can be quite complex with the additional presence of "foster parents". These are thought to have lost their nests to predation and adopted that of another pair, helping in all aspects of the communal life. During February any unmated females leave the group to join flocks in neighbouring territories, after which, pairing takes place.

Since the breeding season they will have been roosting communally in thick cover, often close to the ground. Once the nests are built the roosts break up and the new nests are used.

Long-tailed Tits collect much of their insect food from twigs so they like dense hedgerows and scrub but venture out into more open woodland and among the sparcer trees on Wisley common. In the RHS Garden there is so much scope for them that they can be met with almost anywhere. The largest concentrations tend to be along the River Walk.

In 1985 a pair nested in the privet hedge of the writers' garden, enabling close study of the nest building and territory defence. They were very annoyed with the reflection of light cast from the sun off a window. They took turns to dart along the top of the hedge, drum rapidly on the window and then fly back again. The performance was repeated over and over again when the reflection intruding into their territory refused to budge. It didn't deter them though and a family was successfully fledged.

Coal Tit

The longer bill of the Coal Tit hints at differing survival tactics from some of its relatives. It's used for pushing down into pine needles in search of insects that try to hide in the deep crevices where pine needles join together.

This is a bird that associates freely with conifers and has benefitted from the expansion of forestry. At Wisley the best place by far to see them is through the RHS Pinetum. Just as insect life has adapted to the introduced species of conifer, so has the Coal Tit in its search for food. It also associates freely with the Goldcrest and both species can be found in isolated conifers away from groups or plantations.

Coal Tits also frequent mixed and deciduous woodland, sometimes being the most numerous tit there especially where Marsh and Willow Tits are absent.

In autumn when insects become more scarce the Coal Tit turns to seeds, being particularly fond of beech mast - hence the bill that is not only longer but is also stronger than that of some of its relatives. It needs to be for splitting the hard cases of beech mast and similar seeds.

Although it will use nest boxes, its favoured site is low down near the ground, perhaps among tree roots, or even under ground in holes. In May 1983 a visitor to the RHS Garden brought work to a standstill on the construction of a demonstration garden for television. A Coal Tit was taking food into a cavity behind the partially constructed steps. Sure enough, a pair of Coal Tits had already moved in and built a nest. Staff delayed completing the work until the nestlings safely fledged.

(Coal Tit is one of the ancient bird names. As the Coal Titmouse or Coalmouse it goes right back to the Anglo-Saxon Kolmase.)

139

Blue Tit

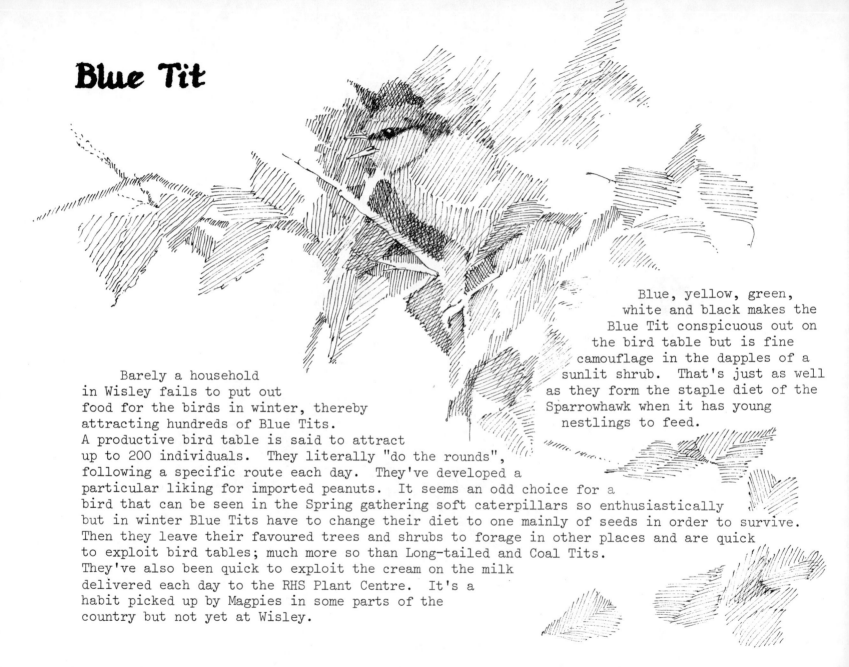

Blue, yellow, green, white and black makes the Blue Tit conspicuous out on the bird table but is fine camouflage in the dapples of a sunlit shrub. That's just as well as they form the staple diet of the Sparrowhawk when it has young nestlings to feed.

Barely a household in Wisley fails to put out food for the birds in winter, thereby attracting hundreds of Blue Tits. A productive bird table is said to attract up to 200 individuals. They literally "do the rounds", following a specific route each day. They've developed a particular liking for imported peanuts. It seems an odd choice for a bird that can be seen in the Spring gathering soft caterpillars so enthusiastically but in winter Blue Tits have to change their diet to one mainly of seeds in order to survive. Then they leave their favoured trees and shrubs to forage in other places and are quick to exploit bird tables; much more so than Long-tailed and Coal Tits. They've also been quick to exploit the cream on the milk delivered each day to the RHS Plant Centre. It's a habit picked up by Magpies in some parts of the country but not yet at Wisley.

In deciduous woodland the Blue Tit is liable to be outnumbered by the Great Tit and in coniferous woodland by the Coal Tit. Villages like Wisley have such high numbers because of all the food that is provided in winter and by the provision of nesting boxes. Blue Tits breed naturally in holes in trees so they adapt to boxes very readily.

Providing boxes is not a new trend at Wisley. Evidently they were already being provided in the RHS Wild Garden by 1907 when their occupation by Blue Tits was recorded.

Blue Tits are also well known for nesting in unexpected places. For example, in 1984 a pair nested in a dustbin behind the RHS Glasshouses. It was so full that the lid was balanced on top but there was just enough room for the nest to be secreted below the rim. The bin was not full with the usual rubbish but with broken glass. The pair successfully raised their brood without causing a devastating cascade of glass.

If that pair caused consternation another pair baffles the staff at the RHS Laboratory each year when they nest in the air ducts. The only apparent means of entry is by squeezing through the tiny holes of the ventilation grills !

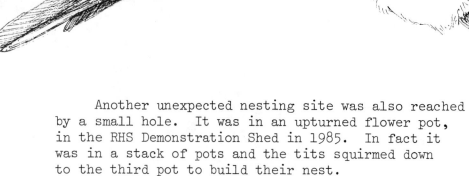

Another unexpected nesting site was also reached by a small hole. It was in an upturned flower pot, in the RHS Demonstration Shed in 1985. In fact it was in a stack of pots and the tits squirmed down to the third pot to build their nest.

Despite all the aid derived from man Blue Tit numbers are not stable. Every now and again the population increases until it errupts into mass movements. That last occurred in 1957 on the Continent. They swarmed into this country and swept up British birds in their movements which also included a return to the Continent.

Great Tit

Continental and British Great Tits lead very different lives. The former are regularly migratory whereas the British Great Tits are largely sedentary. They can be found throughout the year at Wisley, wherever there are trees; from scrub to deciduous woodland, from gardens to conifers. They find a hole to breed in and set up a territory in early April. Thus the young are fledged by early June when food is at its most abundant.

As the season cools into autumn and insect life becomes scarcer, so the Great Tit turns to the year's fruit and then to seeds in order to survive the winter – hence the stout bill. That's ideal for dealing with two favourite seeds – the beech and the hazel nuts. These it will wedge into the bark of a mature tree to hold them steady while the hard shell is hammered away, which produces a sound that is easily confused with that produced by a Nuthatch. For feeding on the ground, the Great Tit is the best adapted of the tits.

In England the Great Tit is not as widespread as the Blue Tit but the population is supplemented by migrants from the Continent which may change the balance. This occurs most noticeably in the winter when the flocks enlarge. Such flocks are usually a mixture of tit species; the core of Great Tits is likely to be all one family. The parents, especially the males, are absent, guarding the breeding territory and will remain so if it is a mild winter, otherwise they have to move out of the woodlands to frequent gardens and bird tables.

Like the Blue Tits they use a whole range of sites for nesting. One nest was found by the RHS Garden staff down inside a hollow metal fence post. The parents dropped in through the open top.

Nest boxes are used regularly.

C. Hawkins 1988

143

Nuthatch

Books with coloured illustrations have a fine subject in the Nuthatch but seeing the real bird in a mature tree is far from easy. Its colouring proves deceptive. Early spring is a good time to find them before the leaves obscure the view. Once the call and song have been learnt they are much easier to find at this time of the year for theirs is one of the more striking sounds of spring.

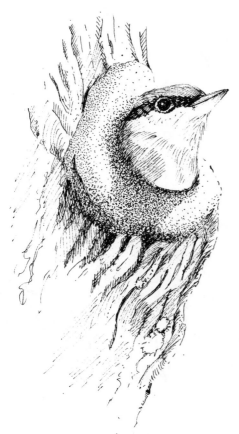

Look wherever there are mature deciduous trees whether isolated in a garden, in a hedgerow or as part of a woodland including mixed woodland. They're usually to be found against the trunk and larger boughs where they search the crevices with their long bills for insect food. It's also a strong bill and with it they hammer off the cases of such seeds as chestnuts, beechnuts and hazelnuts, having first lodged them securely in a crevice. In winter they will take peanuts from garden holders and do the same with those.

In their search for insects they will move both up and down the trunk, facing the way they are going. Even when upside down their hold is achieved entirely with their long claws. The tail is not used at all and so is not stiffened as is the case with Treecreepers and the Woodpeckers. It's an amazing little bird to watch.

The nest is hidden within a hole inside the tree
with the entrance cemented around with mud to leave a
hole only about 3cm in diameter. If they use a nest
box with a tiny hole they still cement round it. Such
a ring of pale dried mud on a tree is a sure sign of
Nuthatch activity.

They are a resident and sedentary bird
becoming very territorial in the winter. At that time
they will join Tit flocks moving through their territory
and travel with them to feed at garden bird tables. At
the RHS Plant Centre they feed off the ground, with Tits
and House Sparrows, when food is put out during hard
weather. They regularly occur at the Label
Department where food is also provided.
Elsewhere in the Garden, Battleston Hill
and the Wild Garden are much used.
They have been recorded from the
Pinetum too. Many visitors
find they need travel no
further than the trees at
the Car Park - a fine
welcome for visitors
from areas where
Nuthatches are
rarities or
absent.

145

Tree Creeper

Usually it's only the ringer who really appreciates the strength of the tail of the Tree Creeper. Even when held in the hand the bird still spreads the feathers and presses them down. Then the power and the special reinforcing of the mid-ribs becomes apparent. This is the secret of the bird's success as it hunts the tree trunks for food. Bracing itself with the tail and clutching the bark with long hooked claws it defies wind and tree movement. When disturbed it takes up this rigid stance, head upwards, awaiting danger to pass. The mottled brown plumage makes for superb camouflage and makes it very difficult to see. That might explain its abscence from the 1909 Wisley report.

The best chances of seeing them are when the nestlings fledge because the family group stays together and make a lot of noise as they keep in contact with one another.

Look for Tree Creepers wherever there are mature trees. On the Continent they seem to prefer conifers whereas in Britain they prefer deciduous trees. Certainly there are more nest sites in a deciduous tree. The bird tucks its nest into clefts and behind loose bark or between the thick stems of ivy. Special nest boxes have also been successfully designed. At Wisley they do frequent the conifers in the RHS Pinetum but you are just as likely to see them in the Wild Garden or on Battleston Hill. The best place to see them is in the trees bordering the river especially near the Pump House.

Despite being very sedentary birds the families do not overpopulate their area due to heavy losses during hard weather. They rely on insect food in the bark which is extracted with their long curved beak. They are the only bird to exploit this source but even so it's not enough to fortify them against prolonged cold.

Jay

The Jay is not very popular among the bird lovers of Wisley for it feeds too readily upon the eggs and nestlings of lesser birds, many of which have a hard time anyway. All the trees around Wisley, whether on the common, in the RHS Garden or about the village, make an ideal habitat for this member of the crow family. It's the one member that still prefers plenty of tree cover.

Gradually it's becoming more tolerant of man and will even make fleeting visits to bird tables. Its more persistent raids upon fruit and vegetables in village gardens do not increase its welcome either. The secret contents of broad bean and pea pods are no secret to the Jay. It doesn't give up until the crop is stripped or thoroughly netted.

In autumn it buries surplus seeds and then returns for them during the winter whenever food is scarce. This proves important ecologically when seeds have no easy means of self-dispersal such as the oak. Without the Jay "planting" acorns and not returning for them it's almost impossible for the oak to spread uphill.

The Jay is a bird of extremes. It can be extremely vocal when it thinks it's at a safe distance but take one by surprise and it flees not only speedily but in silence. A white rump above a black tail is all it's prepared to offer for identification. When it comes to nesting it is highly secretive, not only in the cunning with which it hides its nest in the densest cover it can find but in the silent stealth with which it approaches or leaves the site. Nests are therefore rarely found. Young Jays have been ringed in the RHS Garden but whether they were raised in one of its secluded nooks or whether they flew in from outside, is unknown.

147

Although gardeners are liable
to try and deter the Jay they don't
usually kill it. Persecution from
gamekeepers and farmers has also
declined so numbers have increased
over the last seventy years.

It's basically a sedentary
bird having little cause to move
far as its diet is so varied.
Apart from the eggs, nestlings,
fruit and seeds already mentioned
the Jay eats all manner of
insects and other invertebrate
life. However, in 1983 large
movements did occur. Flocks from
the Continent invaded south and
eastern England. Numbers are
high over there too and so
perhaps, just for once, the food
supplies were running low.

Jays have always
been recorded at Wisley.
Look wherever there
are trees, especially
oaks, in autumn when it's
a good acorn year.

Magpie

So common and conspicuous is the Magpie around Wisley that on most days it would be difficult to explore the area without finding at least one.

They regularly hop around the open spaces in the RHS Garden scavenging for anything edible as they become more and more accepting of man. Unlike the Jay, they are no longer wary nor tree-bound. In fact they are quite brazen about their nesting, often constructing their large nest of twigs in clear view, relying for protection on its height from the ground or the dense twiggy, often thorny, nature of the support. Over the top it builds a roof so the eggs are not visible from above but the Magpie's nest has few predators. Instead it is the smaller song birds' nests that are heavily predated by the Magpie. From this point of view it is unfortunate that the Magpie is increasing in numbers. This is largely due to the decline over the last sixty to seventy years of their being shot by farmers and game-keepers. This reflects the local decline in importance of game rearing and free-range poultry.

Such stockbreeding was much to the benefit of small birds for it was not just the Magpie that was shot but all possible predators, whether birds or certain mammals, from foxes down to the weasel. All these predators now have an easier time – at the expense of the small birds.

As the folklore rhymes record, the Magpies tend to move about in groups. These comprise the offspring of a particular brood. They stay together for about two years. In winter, groups merge together to exploit food sources, to mob other predators and for communal roosting. Such gatherings are primarily from December to April and comprise the immature birds. At certain times up to thirty can be seen in the fields beyond the river. Their mature elders tend to remain in the breeding territory and are often busy nest building by the end of February although egg laying may be delayed until April.

149

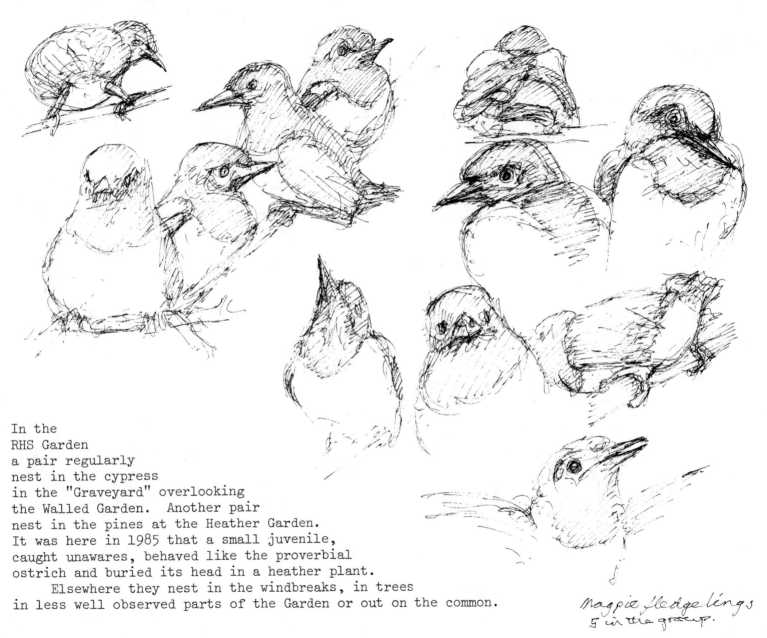

In the
RHS Garden
a pair regularly
nest in the cypress
in the "Graveyard" overlooking
the Walled Garden. Another pair
nest in the pines at the Heather Garden.
It was here in 1985 that a small juvenile,
caught unawares, behaved like the proverbial
ostrich and buried its head in a heather plant.
     Elsewhere they nest in the windbreaks, in trees
in less well observed parts of the Garden or out on the common.

Magpie fledgelings
5 in the group.

150

Fledgelings
which have not
grown their
tail feathers
yet.

151

Jackdaw

The little cock and hen bantam make the Jackdaw look big but it's the smallest of the black crows. It can be just as opportunist as the rest of its family when it comes to finding food and will regularly visit poultry runs in the hope of finding scattered corn. Its normal food is invertebrate life found out in the fields where it often feeds with Rooks. The latter are much larger and lack the grey nape and grey on the side of the cheeks that distinguish the Jackdaw. Come May and the Jackdaws move up into the tree tops to plunder the caterpillars.

Wisley has both fields and trees so it's a good place to seek the Jackdaw. You're unlikely to be disappointed. Small flocks regularly patrol the village, breaking into pairs to go searching for food and then rejoining the flock. They've been doing this around Wisley for at least a hundred years.

They nest communally and one small colony can be found at the village end of Howards Field where they like the poplars. Unfortunately these trees have been slowly losing their tops. Then in the "hurricane" of 1987 a whole tree was brought down and with it two of the nesting holes and a nesting box. By adding these boxes the size of a colony can be increased, providing squirrels don't move in. Jackdaws fill the boxes with sticks. They do the same if they use a chimney. Whatever the size of the cavity they fill it.

During hard winter weather when the ground is frozen too hard for them to dig out grubs the Jackdaws leave Wisley and move west. Numbers eventually build up in Ireland while here in the east flocks from the Continent move through. Frosty weather brings them scavenging around the RHS Car Park and sometimes to bird tables in the village gardens. For most of the year though their cheery chack chack chack can be heard around Wisley, especially before they go to roost.

Rook

The distinctive cawing sound of Rooks has been broadcast so often to evoke thoughts of the English countryside that it has rapidly grown a nostalgia value, even more so since the demise of so many elm trees that held rookeries. Fortunately the rookery at Wisley survives. From the RHS Trials Field it can be seen beyond the A3. It's been in use at least forty years; the 1947 report refers to large numbers of Rooks in the vicinity. In recent years at least twenty nests have been in use.

The Rook is a bird of the farmland and its numbers fluctuate in accordance with farming practice. It does the farmer a great service by ridding the soil, both bare and in pasture, of vast quantities of invertebrate life, such as leather-jackets, which would otherwise harm the crops. Chemical seed dressings are therefore not in the Rooks' favour. When the soil is hidden by tall corn the Rook can turn to a seed-based diet and then so much corn can be devoured that it's rated a serious pest. Little corn is grown around Wisley nowadays so the Rooks are less persecuted than they might be.

They can be seen regularly in the fields opposite the RHS Pinetum, feeding in association with Jackdaws and Carrion Crows. They will all roost together communally (out of the breeding season) after gathering in a pre-roost assembly. Occasionally a rook can be seen scavenging in the Picnic Area beside the RHS Car Park.

Carrion Crow

The big black Carrion Crows can be seen
at any time anywhere around Wisley. Out on
the common, in the RHS Garden, out in the
fields, it exploits all habitats for food
making it one of the commonest birds in
Britain. It has adapted readily to
man and to recent changes in farming
practice. Where there are trees it will
nest high in a fork, where there are not, then
it will nest lower in thick bushes. Being a large and
fearsome bird, few others will predate its nest; even the
squirrel is wary.

Carrion Crows will attack and feed on a wide range of smaller
vertebrates, given the chance, and like the Rook, takes masses of
invertebrates and seeds. It renders a useful service in clearing
carrion, hence its regular appearance along roadsides, seeking
casualties. Unfortunately for the lesser birds, it takes eggs
and nestlings, causing it to be much persecuted in the past by
gamekeepers.

Like the Rook, those around Wisley are largely sedentary
birds. Only the immature or unmated birds wander off into
flocks. They roost with Rooks and Jackdaws in dense woodland.
Similarly, there is rarely an influx of extra birds in winter,
as happens with so many other species. Although Britain does
receive some Continental crows in winter, these are more
likely to be Hooded Crows which rarely venture this far
south.

155

Starling

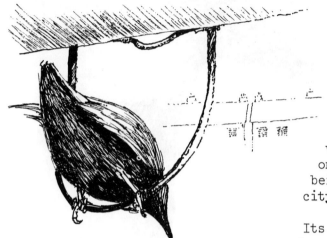

Bobbing around under the eaves, squabbling at the bird bath, greedily gulping food at the bird table, systematically probing lawns or wheeling in great noisy aerobatic flocks, the ordinary old Starling provides a whole range of activities to study and there's much more to learn about it yet. How, for example are feeding flocks synchronised so that they all take off at once and why ? How come the Starling appears so successful nowadays while last century it was a rarity and even at the beginning of this century it was still quite local in its distribution ? Now it's one of the most widespread and common of British birds, being equally at home in remote rural areas and in busy city centres.

Its first priority is to find a good supply of food. It prefers invertebrate life and to hunt for this it is provided with a strong sharply pointed beak, long enough to penetrate below the soil surface. It leaves quite sizeable holes in a lawn ! In the autumn it is very fond of fruit, from small berries up to windfall apples. After these have all gone it turns to seeds and food on bird tables.

Its second priority is to find good breeding sites and for this it seeks out cavities - any sort of cavity. The modern Starling doesn't seem fussy about anything ! During the second half of April the first clutch will be laid and soon the loud squawking of the nestlings will belie the location of the nest, if large deposits of white excrement below the hole haven't done so already. The young leave the nest in early May and a second brood is ready to leave in about another eight weeks.

As the days shorten, numbers are swollen by large influxes from the Continent. Very handsome the Starling can be too, in new iridescent glossy black all smartly speckled.

Wisley was one of the places where the Starling was already common at the beginning of the century. Today, flocks can be regularly watched swirling above the sewage works, before dropping down to feed on the filter beds. Then they're up and swirling again, never still for long.

Beside the riverbank they nest in natural holes in the trees. In the RHS Garden they use the nest boxes provided for them. Fledging seems to coincide with the farmer cutting the field opposite the Pinetum for silage. That exposes the invertebrates that have built up under cover of the crop. Starlings arrive in their hundreds, showing just how successful they are today. The noise is deafening as they fly back into the Garden to pause for a rest in the trees before going back for another fill. The grandest nest site is in the top of the urns on the corners of the Walled Garden where visitors can very easily watch the parents arriving with bills crammed with food.

Starling nest site – one of the urns on top of the wall of the RHS Walled Garden.

House Sparrow

The House Sparrow is Wisley's most internationally well-known bird. It is also the one most closely associated with man. It's invariably a man-made structure that provides some sort of crevice or cavity in which the House Sparrow breeds and with up to four broods per year, it certainly breeds. The mortality rate is high, however.

Without man's support the House Sparrow builds a large untidy domed nest in a bush, even at Wisley where there are plenty of buildings. Here too it has been compromising by building such a nest in a creeper against a wall.

It may be small but it's extremely determined, whether at noisily defending its own nest or at driving others, such as Swallows, House Martins and Tits, out of theirs, so that the House Sparrows can take over the nest for their own use. With nest boxes this can be overcome by reducing the diameter of the hole to 2.8cm or less.

Communal by nature, they feed in flocks on seed and can thus do serious damage to a corn crop, making them an agricultural pest. Gardeners are not always very pleased with them either, especially when they dust-bath in a seed bed but on the other hand they do devour vast quantities of weed seeds. From the Tits they've learnt how to hang and feed from peanut hoppers and how to raid milk bottles for the cream.

They're almost totally sedentary, with only a small dispersal of young birds in the autumn and again in the spring for breeding.

House Sparrows and Starlings
outside the studio window.

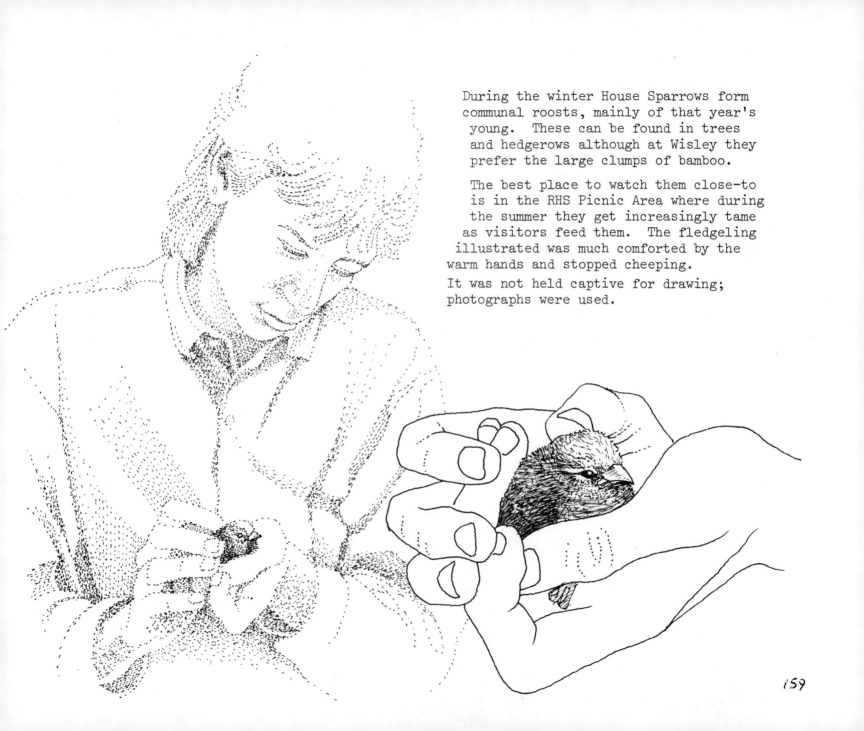

During the winter House Sparrows form communal roosts, mainly of that year's young. These can be found in trees and hedgerows although at Wisley they prefer the large clumps of bamboo.

The best place to watch them close-to is in the RHS Picnic Area where during the summer they get increasingly tame as visitors feed them. The fledgeling illustrated was much comforted by the warm hands and stopped cheeping.

It was not held captive for drawing; photographs were used.

159

Tree Sparrow

This is one of the Wisley birds that's
in decline. Until the early 1960s there
were good numbers in residence - a flock
of 140 was recorded on the common on
August 13th 1961 - but then numbers began
to fall although it held on as a breeding
species until the early 1970s. Since then
records have only caught it on migration for,
although sedentary by nature, it joins mixed
flocks of finches and buntings in cold weather
when there are movements towards the east coast.
Just such a flock visited the sewage works in the
autumn of 1986. The species in a mixed flock do not
separate in the evening but roost communally in thick shrubs.

A possible reason for the decline is the use of agricultural
herbicides to combat weeds. It's the seeds of the weeds
that form the basis of the Tree Sparrow's diet. The more
unfamiliar the Tree Sparrow becomes the more likely it is to be
mistaken for a House Sparrow and thus be under-recorded. It's
smaller and far more secretive than the House Sparrow but best
distinguished by its chocolate coloured crown.

Most often it is seen in old orchards and woodland where the trees
are mature enough to provide nesting holes. For these the Tree Sparrow
has to compete with the Tits. Occasionally they take to old Sand
Martin burrows or snuggle the nest between the mature stems of
climbers such as Ivy.

161

Chaffinch

Its name comes from its old habit of frequenting threshing yards to feed on the chaff but those farming practices have gone. Now it maintains itself on general weed seeds and cereals to which its bill is well suited. It doesn't have the specialised development of the Hawfinch or Crossbill, nor, to a lesser extent, the Redpoll and Siskin. Its diet was fine until toxic seed dressings caused a serious decline in its numbers by the early 1960s, levelling off during the mid decade. Now that farmers are less liberal with toxic chemicals the Chaffinch numbers have recovered and it is probably the commonest bird around Wisley.

It likes its terrain to have plenty of trees and shrubs. There they set up breeding territories in February but it's not until April that the female builds her exquisite nest, carefully camouflaged and thoroughly hidden. It's so successful that even with only one brood a year high numbers are maintained.

Local birds tend to be sedentary but in autumn their numbers are supplemented with influxes from Scandinavia. These form large flocks and roost communally unlike the local birds which roost in their old territory. Scandinavian migrants tend to be a little larger and a little paler and mostly female.

Scandinavian males prefer to remain guarding their territories hence "coelebs" as their specific scientific name which means bachelor. In Surrey their local name is the affectionate "chaffie" or older still, "caffey". Oddly "caffincher" has also been recorded which is more often found in northern dialects.

In the RHS Garden they nest regularly in the climbers of both the Walled and the Model Gardens aswell as in the more compact growing conifers scattered through the Pinetum. On occasions they have moved into the Glasshouses to nest in the climbers there. During the breeding season they can be found throughout the Garden but when cold weather sets in they join the thrushes in the Orchard to feast on the windfalls. They also frequent the Picnic Area beside the Car Park to see what pickings the visitors have left.

Brambling

This is one of the lesser known
winter migrants, arriving in
October/November. Its first
appearance on the Wisley records
was not until 1955. It may get
overlooked because it freely
associates with Chaffinches which
it resembles at first glance.
Closer observation reveals the
distinctive white rump of the
Brambling which isn't shared with the
Chaffinch.

Their favourite food is the beech mast so
the better the mast year the better are
the chances of seeing them. Failing that,
watch for them among Chaffinches flocked in
the fields seeking cereals and weed seeds or
in the RHS Orchard taking advantage of the
windfalls. They have also been recorded in the
RHS Pinetum and even more often from the market garden
ground next to the new RHS Arboretum. Numbers vary from
year to year according to the mast yield and following
national trends.

As evening approaches they stay with the Chaffinches,
coming in from all around to join a pre-roost flock
before moving in for a night's shelter in conifers or
Rhododendrons.

Greenfinch

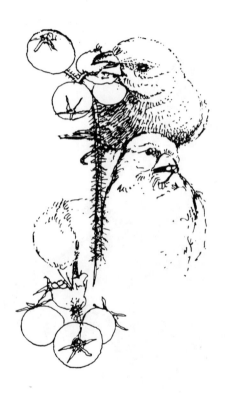

Known to the old Surrey folk as the Green Linnet or Bey, this is an example of a bird extending its range. Originally, in this country, it was a bird of woodland edges but it has since moved out into thorny scrub and young conifer plantations and now into farmland and gardens. In the last it has learnt to exploit bird tables and to take peanuts from hoppers. This helps sustain populations in winter when they have cleared most of the farmland etc. of their favourite seeds. Otherwise they become partial migrants, moving off south and west towards the coast. A few even go off to the Continent instead of the usual story of their birds coming to Britain, although a few of their Greenfinches do indeed come over.

As early as January the birds start singing and the male can be seen displaying to the female. It's not until April that she gets on with nest building, receiving little help from her mate. For nesting they remain in their small groups, choosing a colonial nest site which makes it easier to find, especially as the young clamour loudly for food. The usual trick of tracing adults with food back to their nest doesn't work so well with Greenfinches because they have the habit of feeding their young on regurgitated food. As egg laying may not begin until May the second brood is still in the nest as late as August. Perhaps these are the ones that suffer most in severe weather when numbers certainly fall but the species is capable of a quick recovery.

Around Wisley they are well distributed but not in large numbers. Severe weather brings them into the village gardens but the best place to seek them is in the pine windbreak of Howards Field. There you'll hear their distinctive wheezing call.

Greenfinches
feeding on
rugosa roses.
17-11-1987

165

Goldfinch

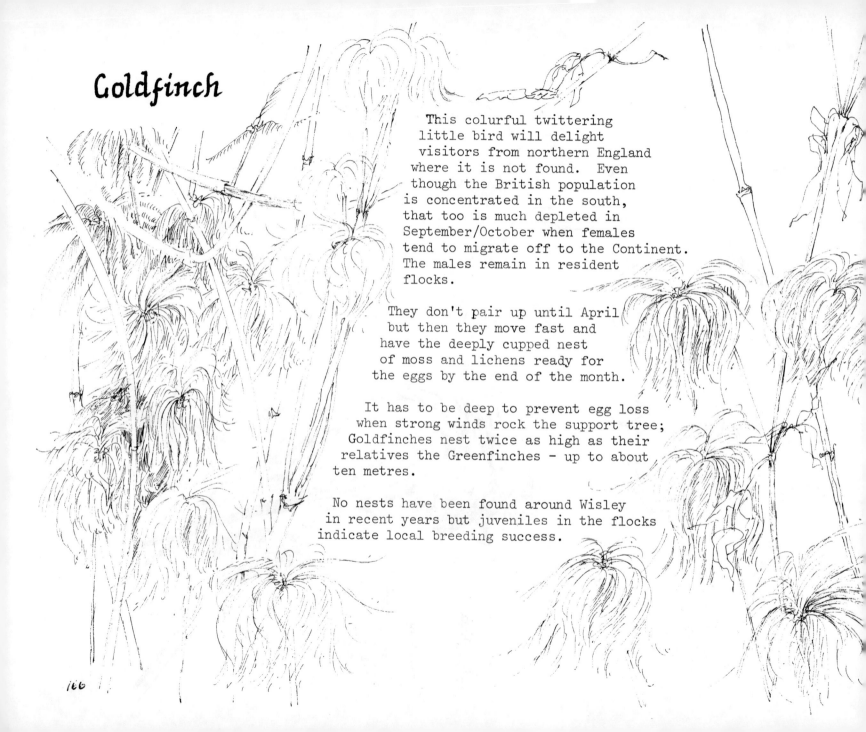

This colourful twittering
little bird will delight
visitors from northern England
where it is not found. Even
though the British population
is concentrated in the south,
that too is much depleted in
September/October when females
tend to migrate off to the Continent.
The males remain in resident
flocks.

They don't pair up until April
but then they move fast and
have the deeply cupped nest
of moss and lichens ready for
the eggs by the end of the month.

It has to be deep to prevent egg loss
when strong winds rock the support tree;
Goldfinches nest twice as high as their
relatives the Greenfinches - up to about
ten metres.

No nests have been found around Wisley
in recent years but juveniles in the flocks
indicate local breeding success.

When it's a hot summer,
ripening plenty of food,
the Goldfinches capitalise
upon it and raise several broods.
Their small parties or "charms"
can be seen along the roadsides,
out in the farmland or about
waste areas, gathering seed.

They have specially long bills
to probe for seeds other birds
cannot reach, such as in teasel
and thistle heads but they're also
fond of dandelion seed.

Being so selective there is no advantage
in joining mixed flocks in winter to
search for food although around Wisley
they can be found with Redpolls and Siskins
feeding on birch and alder cones.

Apart from these trees attracting them,
the best place to find Goldfinches in winter
is in the RHS Orchard; flocks of up to 100 were
there in January 1985. Otherwise look round the
village allotments or in gardens that have not been
tidied up for the winter. Goldfinches haven't begun visiting bird tables yet.

167

Siskin

Siskins have traditionally been birds of the north, feeding on alder, birch and conifer seed. Then the spread of conifer afforestation this century enabled the Siskin to extend its range enormously. It was first added to the Wisley list in the 1955 RHS Garden Club Journal.

It still breeds in the north but moves south afterwards, in search of food, usually reaching Wisley in October and staying until March. Flocks vary in size from 20 to 200, frequenting the river areas in search of alder and larch, but much larger flocks can be seen in the alders along the Wey Navigation towpath from the Anchor Pub up to Ockham Mill.

Numbers are supplemented by flocks from Scandinavia and Russia. On Wisley Common 450 were recorded on March 24th 1963. Nevertheless they can be easily overlooked because they feed high in the tree tops, all the time there are supplies of seed. When that begins to run out or when winds are too strong they will drop down to feed lower and if gales have shaken the seed down to the ground then the Siskins will come down too to collect it. Once this supply is exhausted they will explore gardens and will now take peanuts from holders or feed on suspended fat.

Look out also for the very distinctive swirling twittering masses that reel around the tree tops if they've been disturbed.

Linnet

Linseed oil sounds familiar enough but the days when Surrey had plenty of lin or flax fields are no more. The bird that fed there and got the name Linnet still survives. It was common enough, like the Goldfinch, for them both to be trapped for the cage bird trade. That was stopped ealier this century (primarily by efforts from Surrey) but any recovery in Linnet numbers was again reduced by lack of food as modern herbicides controlled the weeds in the fields that the Linnets fed upon. Modern farming practices and larger fields all work against the Linnet.

Fortunately there are enough rough weedy places around Wisley to support a small resident population, even to keeping them well through severe weather which takes a toll of so many other species. They flock together in the winter - the more eyes to spot food the better - and can be seen around the allotments and the RHS Fruit Fields. Sometimes they're in mixed flocks of seed eaters and if disturbed all the Linnets tend to keep together. Similarly when mixed flocks share a communal winter roost the Linnets stay together. Thorn and gorse bushes are preferred for this but when the flocks break up for the breeding season they adopt any scrubby cover that will provide a secure nest site within four metres of the ground. Village hedgerows have been used but breeding has not been proved for every year.

Laying begins in April when many return from over-wintering in France and Spain, and with two or more broods the adults are still busy in August. When the female brings food to the nest the male comes with her and stands guard. Come September and October many return to France and Spain but numbers at Wisley increase as birds move in from districts short of food, maybe from as far as Scandinavia.

Redpoll

Like the Siskin, this
is another bird traditionally
of the northern birchwoods
and moors, only coming south
in search of food during the
severe winters.

Increased afforestation
has encouraged it to move
more regularly into the
southern regions where
there are also plenty of
birch trees to provide it
with winter seed. As more
and more heathland becomes
invaded by birch so the little
Redpoll prospers. It likes
it even better than the
Siskin and often stays to
breed, although nesting at
Wisley has not been proven
in the last few years.

It was first recorded at Wisley
in the 1955 report, ahead of the
general increase that occurred
in the early 1960s and through
to the mid 1970s. It is still
not a particularly common bird
here, even in the winter,
unless it's one of the
exceptional peak years.
Numbers depend very much
upon the severity of the
weather and upon the levels
of food available.

Birch seed is its chief food
but at Wisley they like larch
aswell, and can be seen in
flight across the village
from the larches beyond Howards
Field to the allotments where
they gather to feed on weed seeds.

They also join Siskins on
alder cones. When supplies
of food run low they move
on, to the south and to
the west.

♀

Crossbill

With its hooked bill, crossing and overlapping, this is the most specialised of the finches. The design is specifically for twisting the seeds out of pine and spruce cones, so again this is another species that has prospered with increases in afforestation and the degeneration of heathland into mixed woodland with pines of cone bearing age.

Supplies of such seed peak early in the year rather than the autumn, so egg laying is very early, in February, so that there should be good supplies of food for the young. Nevertheless, these develop so slowly that a second brood may not be possible until well into April. Young Crossbills take about 45 days to become independent of their parents (nearly a week more than other finches). This is because their diet of seed and mucus provided by their parents is not enriched with the proteins from insect life that other birds supplement the diet of the nestlings with.

The Common Crossbill has not been recorded as breeding at Wisley. It is a regular visitor though. They have developed a migration pattern that is not seasonal but which occurs only when numbers reach a level too high to be maintained by the local supply of food. Then they move off to seek fresh feeding grounds. It is during these years of irruptions that large numbers arrive in this country and it is in the aftermath of these irruptions that Crossbills are most likely to be seen at Wisley. Large numbers were recorded in 1962 for example. The very first record of Crossbills at Wisley was in 1947 and since then they have occurred regularly. The largest sighting was of 107 on July 17th 1960. Numbers obviously depend upon breeding success but that depends upon the fruiting success of the conifers so that even regular breeding sites depend upon influxes from the Continent to keep them viable.

Wisley sightings are usually around Boldermere, with fewer birds recorded at any one time out on the common. Look also where there is surface water as Crossbills, like other seed eaters, get little moisture from their food and must come down to drink.

Bullfinch

Notorious among fruit farmers and gardeners, for stripping trees of their flower buds, the Bullfinch resorts to such food to sustain them through shortages of their natural food. That's chiefly seeds, with those of the ash tree a firm favourite, but supplemented with insect life, especially for the nestlings, to provide extra supplies of protein. In years when there is a good supply of natural food there is little damage to man's crops.

In the 1909 report we read that they were regularly shot as a pest in the RHS Garden. By the time the 1955 report was produced the increased number of Bullfinches breeding locally was almost welcomed. They still do a certain amount of damage in the RHS Garden but are probably less common there now than in 1955, having been driven out by the increasing numbers of visitors. Certainly they are no longer persecuted. In other areas large numbers are trapped by fruit farmers in the autumn, permissable in law under certain conditions, because the bird can be such a serious pest.

At Wisley they can be enjoyed not only in the RHS Fruit Fields but along the river bordering Howards Field and out on the common. Originally it was a bird associated with such scrubby places and at the edges of woodland. Now it's just as likely to be seen along hedgerows and in gardens.

172

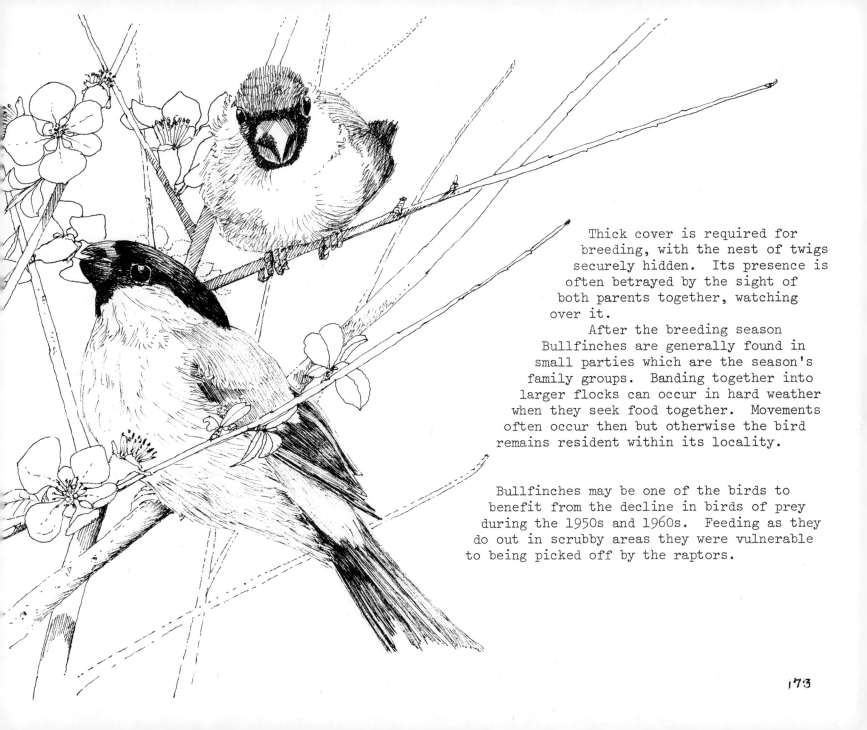

Thick cover is required for
breeding, with the nest of twigs
securely hidden. Its presence is
often betrayed by the sight of
both parents together, watching
over it.
    After the breeding season
Bullfinches are generally found in
small parties which are the season's
family groups. Banding together into
larger flocks can occur in hard weather
when they seek food together. Movements
often occur then but otherwise the bird
remains resident within its locality.

Bullfinches may be one of the birds to
benefit from the decline in birds of prey
during the 1950s and 1960s. Feeding as they
do out in scrubby areas they were vulnerable
to being picked off by the raptors.

Hawfinch

The King of Finches is no doubt an under-recorded species, being quiet and secretive, living high in the tree tops where it is difficult to see.

It's immediately recognisable by its massive beak, strong enough for cracking open its favourite food - cherry stones. It is not very kind to the fingers of an unwary bird ringer either ! Fruiting cherry trees, whether in gardens or orchards, are therefore worthwhile watching for the chance of seeing this beautiful bird. Look particularly in the highest branches.

Hawfinches have been recorded at Wisley ever since 1909. In 1947 their status was described as an autumn/winter visitor, reflecting their tendency to flock together then, changing from their usual sedentary nature to roving around in small flocks looking for food. Chances of spotting them are then increased. Thus, for a few years, they took to stripping the seeds from the hornbeams outside the new RHS Glasshouses but this seems to have ceased. It's always worth checking though. Hawfinches have never been a frequent visitor to Wisley so sightings are likely to be pure chance, like the one spotted along by the canal on February 4th 1985.

It nests up high too, in oaks and sycamores and old fruit trees, only occasionally using overgrown hedges. Watching its family life is very difficult as it's even more secretive at this time. Often it's only when the young are fledged and become noticeably vocal that there's any indication of breeding and such has not been recorded at Wisley.

Like their relatives the bullfinches etc. the Hawfinch builds a nest of twigs rather than one of soft materials preferred by Goldfinches and Chaffinches. Not until the end of May are the eggs laid - after the leaves have unfurled to hide the nest from view. The nest may be in isolation or in small colonies.

175

178   yellowhammers.

Yellowhammer

A walk round the open
areas of Wisley common
is almost certain to flush
out a Yellowhammer.

It used to be very common there
but is less so nowadays, perhaps
because the scrub is invading too
much. It needs trees and bushes to
sing from but otherwise it's a bird
of the open country. It has
adapted well to changing
farming practices but it
benefits most when food
is spread on the fields
for cattle in winter.
Then whole flocks can
be seen descending
upon the easy pickings.

The Yellowhammer is a bunting
but the name Yellow Bunting is
going out of use. It is not a
lark but has been known as the
Writing Lark or the Scribbler,
in the past in Surrey, from the
black squiggles on its eggs.

The population is basically sedentary
but flocking in severe weather and
then becoming more tolerant of man.
Otherwise they seek the quieter,
open, dry areas of Wisley for their
breeding. Look for them on the
common, in the new RHS Arboretum
and along the farm hedges. Nowhere
is the population very high but the
Yellowhammer has always been a breeding
species during the period under review.

They feed communally and will roost communally
but when it comes to breeding they establish
very definite territories and any
intruding Yellowhammer is most
decidedly driven off by the
male, resplendent with his
bright yellow head. They
nest low down in cover,
whether in a hedge bottom,
brambles or bracken, even in
ditches. The Wisley birds seem
to like hiding their nests in
the vegetation hanging down into
drainage channels, the nest itself
often being below general ground
level.

Reed Bunting

The fishermen sitting quietly on the riverbank in one of the more isolated locations have the best chances of seeing this bird in its main habitat. Somewhere there, hidden in the base of some clump of the waterside vegetation, it will nest, and has done so throughout the review period. When the population exceeds the possible number of breeding territories the Reed Bunting moves out into the drier areas and then comes into competition with the Yellowhammer.

The best chances of seeing one at Wisley are therefore in quiet areas adjacent to water. Then, in early summer, you may come upon one, beak crammed with waterside insects for its nestlings, awaiting you to leave the vicinity of the nest. Stray too close and it will distract you by pretending to be injured. Ignore it and move on; all will be well.

In hard weather, however, it can be seen on the farmland, waste ground or at the sewage works, in its search for food. As dusk approaches watch for them returning to the waterside to roost in thick vegetation. Some are now coming into the village gardens to feed from bird tables. One, in the writers' garden, had been ringed at Ripley, (one of the neighbouring villages).

178

Corn Bunting

Corn Bunting by name and by nature but with little corn being grown around Wisley it is not surprising that this is only a scarce resident, as in the rest of Surrey. Its presence is therefore important, especially as it breeds here.

Even in the major cereal districts of the country it is declining. This is probably due to changes in farming practice, with the abandonment of traditional cropping rotations. Autumn sown rather than spring sown corn means that the crop is not at the right stage to synchronise with the Corn Bunting's breeding cycle. They lay their eggs directly into a depression in the cornfield but, failing this, will turn to scrub and that's where Wisley can make a greater contribution. There are records from both the common and from the arable fields bordering the A3 south of the RHS Garden. Such places also provide the bushes, fences and pylons it uses for song perches. They can also be heard flying over the district, presumably on their way to roost.

In winter they flock together to seek food and to roost in scrub communally. Such flocks can be substantial. Then, as early as January, singing begins; males and females pair off and prepare for another breeding season. Eggs are not laid until late May or even later.

Corn Buntings do not appear in the Wisley records until 1948. At present they are declining.

Coal Tit Studies — Wisley.

180

Wisley's Rarities
and
Birds From The Past

— Wheatear

BLACK-THROATED DIVER

Rare winter visitor to the county with most records coming from the larger stretches of water, particularly for the period between 1954/5 to 1957/8. It was during that same period that a single juvenile was recorded at Wisley in 1955. (RHS Garden Club Journal, 1955; no details given).

BLACK-NECKED GREBE

Uncommon annual winter visitor to the county with the numbers of those wintering having increased since the early 1960s. Prior to that, records were normally of single birds. Thus one was seen on Boldermere Lake on 18th December 1960, (Surrey Bird Report).

GREYLAG GOOSE

Very scarce winter visitor to the county. Obvious confusion arises between genuine wild birds and the increasing feral birds of domestic poultry origin. The only record is from 1909 when they flew in V formation over the RHS Garden but no further details were given; (RHS Garden Club Journal, 1909).

SNOW GOOSE

Feral species with two records for the Wisley area. In 1985 five birds flew over on May 4th which had been recorded locally for several weeks (Birds of Wisley, 1985) and then a couple of years later the writers spotted one with Canada Geese flying over the RHS Garden on 10th February.

BAR-HEADED GOOSE

On September 9th 1985 a single bird of this feral species paused briefly on Boldermere Lake and made the first record to date. It was probably the same bird which appeared with a large flock of Canada Geese on the London reservoirs in the August/September of that year. (Birds of Wisley, 1985).

EGYPTIAN GOOSE

A feral species with a single record for the Wisley area, for February 9th 1964 when one appeared on Boldermere Lake, (Surrey Bird Report).

BUZZARD

Scarce passage migrant and winter visitor to the county. It used to breed as a result of an introduced population. Look out for them in particular from March-April and September-Oct. First appeared on the Wisley list in 1955 but no details were given. In 1959 a secondary flight feather was found on Wisley common; (Surrey Bird Report).

greylags - feral.

MERLIN

Rare passage migrant and winter visitor to the county with only a single record for the Wisley area. In 1980 the writers recorded a male chasing House Sparrows in front of the Plant Centre at the RHS Garden.

HOBBY

Summer migrant which is occasionally spotted between May and September. Visitors may not have far to go to see this rarity as it has been recorded chasing the House Martins hawking over the RHS Car Park. It first appeared on the records on July 27th 1963.

WATER RAIL

A winter visitor in small numbers and one which is known to have stayed on to breed in the county. It is a notoriously secretive bird and is no doubt under-recorded. In 1966 one was recorded at Wisley on 23rd January and two on 23rd October. (Surrey Bird Report).

CORNCRAKE

Known in Surrey as the Daker or Daker Hen, the Wisley population has suffered serious decline this century as has the rest of the County. In the 1909 report it was recorded as being frequently heard but with the 1946 report comes the last record of its attempted breeding. It has not been mentioned since.

Wryneck

185

Wryneck

DUNLIN

Passage migrant and regular winter visitor to the county but the only report for Wisley comes from the 1955 RHS Garden Club Journal which reported them as recorded in the last forty years but gave no further details.

GREAT SNIPE

In Birds of Surrey 1900-1970 the Great Snipe was recorded as having been seen on a few occasions but none was well authenticated. It was added to the Wisley list in 1956 from a recording, with no details,in the RHS Garden Journal, 1956.

GOLDEN PLOVER

Reasonably regular winter visitor and passage migrant through the county, with flocks of up to one hundred recorded. Wisley is not a good place to seek them though. In 1908 they were recorded in the RHS Garden (RHS Garden Club Journal,1909) and in 1966 there were two with Lapwings on the common on 20th November, (Surrey Bird Report).

CURLEW

A passage migrant and winter visitor but one which occasionally stays on to breed. It first appears in the 1955 report which states that it had been present previous to that. The only other report is for seven on August 30th 1959, (Surrey Bird Report).

KNOT

Scarce passage migrant and winter visitor to the county with the only report for Wisley being an amazing total of fifty flying over the village at dusk. That was on August 23rd 1968, (Surrey Bird Report).

REDSHANK

Scarce breeding species in Surrey but more often a passage migrant and winter visitor. First bred in the county in 1910 and by the 1950s was breedi at Wisley's sewage farm, according to Birds in Surrey 1900-1970. In 1959 a pair nested in a pasture on Wisley common but the nest was destroyed by ploughing, (Surrey Bird Report).

LITTLE TERN

Scarce passage migrant in the county and only recorded at Wisley on August 22nd 1959 when there were two by the River Wey, (Surrey Bird Report).

RING NECKED PARAKEET

Feral species added to the British list in 1983 having established itself from introductions and escapes. Has bred in the county and appeared at Wisley several times in the last five years.

GREENSHANK

Regular passage migrant, more often seen in the autumn than in the spring. Added to the Wisley list in 1956 but no details were given, (RHS Garden Journal, 1956).

GREEN SANDPIPER

Only two recordings for Wisley even though it is a regular passage migrant through the county. Two birds were seen on the common on February 12th 1961 (Surrey Bird Report) and on January 5th 1985 a single bird was flushed from a muddy inlet on the River Wey. It flew upstream, calling, (Birds of Wisley 1985).

COMMON TERN

The 1956 RHS Garden Club Journal records the sighting of two but no details were given. Regular passage migrant through the county, being recorded in both spring and autumn.

Curlew

SHORT EARED OWL

Occasional winter visitor to the county and might be a passage migrant but the only Wisley record is for one seen on the common on 29th November 1958 (Surrey Bird Report).

WRYNECK

Formerly known in Surrey as the Pee Bird, from its loud call and in the days when this was a common summer resident. Since then the bird has declined sharply in Britain. There are no records since 1947 when the RHS Garden Club Journal reported a few were nesting in holes in trees but were not often seen. Then in 1959 one was seen on September 13th (Surrey Bird Report). Up until 1940 it was common and quite ready to use nesting boxes.

WOODLARK

Scarce species in the county with a local breeding distribution. Numbers have fluctuated during the century, starting low but building up from the 1920s to peak in the 1950s and being recorded at Wisley for the first time in 1949 (RHS Garden Club Journal. The Surrey Bird Report then has entries for 1957, 1958, 1959 and 1961 for no more than two pairs at a time but including breeding. No reports after 1961 as localities were kept secret due to the bird going into rapid decline after the severe winter of 1962-3.

WHITE WAGTAIL

Scarce but annual passage migrant through the county with the only Wisley record being for three birds seen on the common on May 19th 1959.

BLACK REDSTART

Regular passage migrant through the county, rarely staying for the summer but is an occasional winter visitor. The writers recorded a female at the sewage works in December 1986 and then in the following March there was a female, watched for some two hours, on the village allotments. No other records available.

REDSTART

Regular passage migrant through the county but also a regular summer visitor, breeding in a number of localities, including Wisley. In 1948 one was found on Battleston Hill and subsequently found feeding young on the common, (RHS Garden Club Journal). From From 1949 to 1961 it was listed as present and in 1962 they were paired on the common and in the RHS Garden.

Black Redstart

188

WHINCHAT

Very scarce summer visitor to the county and passage migrant having declined dramatically since 1900 so that breeding is no longer an annual event. There are no breeding records at all for Wisley but since 1964 such information has been kept secret. The RHS Garden Club Journal records it as present on the dry common in 1909 and in 1947-9 when it was also to be seen in the Pinetum and was still locally present in 1955. The Surrey Bird Report continues our knowledge with three reported on the common on August 30th 1959 and a female at the sewage works in 1964.

STONECHAT

Locally distributed breeding species in the county with numbers fluctuating in accordance with the severity of the winters. It appears never to have been recorded breeding at Wisley. The RHS Garden Club Journal reports them as present on the dry common in 1909 and again in 1947 when they were also using the Pinetum but there are no Wisley records after that date.

Redstarts

WHEATEAR

Regular passage migrant in small numbers in the county and one which may occasionally stay to breed. Appeared on the Wisley list in 1955 with the comment that it had not occured previously and appears not to have done so since; no details given.

GRASSHOPPER WARBLER

Localised breeding species and passage migrant through the county, including Wisley common. The RHS Garden Club Journal lists it as present in 1955 followed by four records in the Surrey Bird Report: one on the common in 1958 and on April 28th 1962; one singing on the common 5th August 1972 and again some time in 1974. Breeding has not been confirmed but one record is from a time when territory was perhaps being held.

SEDGE WARBLER

Summer visitor to the county breeding in resonable numbers and also passing through on passage. At Wisley there is no particularly suitable habitat to attract it, although areas within the sewage farm may have been used and it is from here that recent reports have come. First added to the Wisley list 1956.

REED WARBLER

Another summer visitor breeding in
reasonable numbers in the county
but for which there is no really
favourable habitat at Wisley.
In 1909 the RHS Garden Club
Journal records them as present
in the reed beds along the River
Wey but reported in 1955 that they
were no longer present. One was
then seen beside the river on 20th
April 1958 (Surrey Bird Report).

WOOD WARBLER

Localised breeding species in
the county and passage migrant.
First mention at Wisley comes from
the 1949 RHS Garden Club Journal
which recorded its continued presence
in 1955. From the Surrey Bird Report
we learn that they were present on the
common during the breeding seasons of
1971 and 1974. In 1986 they were
singing from the entrance to the
Pinetum next to the Pump House.

FIRECREST

 Increasing and breeding in some
parts of the county but there's
only one record for Wisley and that's
its inclusion on the 1955 list.
This is rather surprising as there
would seem to be suitable habitat
at Wisley. It certainly attracts Goldcrests.

PIED FLYCATCHER

 Rare visitor, moving through on
 migration. On April 21st 1970 a
 single male was seen on Wisley
 common (Surrey Bird Report) and on
 April 25th 1985 there was a male in
 the trees along the River Walk in the
 RHS Garden (Birds of Wisley).

MARSH TIT

 Breeding species in the county although in
 fewer numbers than Blue, Great or Coal Tits.
 It likes scrub, whether dry or damp, so the
 common ought to provide suitable habitat but
 this is not the case. It was listed in 1949
 and in 1955 but has not been recorded since.

WILLOW TIT

 Not recognised as a separate species until
 about a hundred years ago, was first recorded
 in Surrey in 1910 and first recorded at Wisley
 on the 1955 list. Similar in status to the
 Marsh Tit and also curiously absent. It prefers
 damp birch and alder wood with rotten trunks
 for nesting in and there are several such
 localities around Wisley - but no Willow Tits.

GOLDEN ORIOLE

Very rare visitor to the county but added to the
Wisley list in 1948 but with the comment that this
was an American species and needed further checkin
It remained on the list in 1955 with the name of
the recorder so presumably it was checked and
accepted; (RHS Garden Club Journal).

PARROT CROSSBILL

A very rare visitor to the county with only one report for the 1900s coming from the Wisley area, when up to four were thought to be present, one of which was ringed on May 15th 1963, (British Birds).

CIRL BUNTING

Until recently a very rare resident in the county but has now almost certainly gone completely. It was recorded in the Wisley area on one occasion. The Surrey Bird Report records that a pair were found breeding in an elm hedge on May 18th 1959.

Male Stonechat

IMPORTANT

All species known to have occurred at Wisley have been listed in this survey but in some cases information has been witheld so as not to endanger the species further.

Readers are reminded that in general it is a criminal offence to harm our British birds and that includes causing disturbance, particularly at their nest sites, even for a quick peep or to photograph.

When information about nesting has been given in this book it is to enhance the readers' understanding and appreciation of what is happening around them. Please do not allow it to encourage any transgression of the law.

Similarly, the mention of a location in this book does not mean that it has public access.

THE GREAT STORM - 16th/17th October 1987
This changed some areas dramatically, such as Battleston Hill in the RHS Garden. Some bird species will perhaps benefit from the increase in open space while others will decline with the loss of tree cover. These changes will need careful observation for when this survey is updated or another is undertaken.

A sheltered corner
of the RHS Garden
in winter.

190

INDEX

Blackbird 14, 20, 76, 107-10, 118
Blackcap 14, 17, 124, 126-8
Brambling 14, 163
Buntings 14, 160
  " Cirl 189
  " Corn 179
  " Reed 11, 15, 178
Buzzard 182
Chiffchaff 17, 128-9
Coot 10, 56-7
Cormorant 14, 34
Corncrake 183
Crossbill 17, 162, 171
  " Parrot 189
Crow, Carrion 154-5
Cuckoo 75-6, 104
Curlew 184-5
Diver, Black-throated 182
Dove, Collared 15, 72-3
  " Stock 22, 70
  " Turtle 74
Dunlin 184
Dunnock 15, 76, 104
Fieldfare 108, 110-11
Finches 14, 15, 160, 165
  " Bull- 172-4
  " Chaff- 162-3, 174
  " Gold- 166-7, 169, 174
  " Green- 15, 164-6
  " Haw- 17, 162, 174-5
Firecrest 188
Flycatcher, Pied 30, 188

Flycatcher, Spotted 21, 134-5
Gadwall 46
Garganey 46
Goldcrest 9, 15, 17, 132-3, 138, 188
Golden Oriole 188
Goosander 46
Goose, Bar-headed 183
  " Canada 10, 16, 38-40, 45, 182
  " Egyptian 182
  " Greylag 182
  " Snow 182
Grebe, Black-necked 182
  " Great Crested 32-3
  " Little 32
Greenshank 185
Gulls 11, 14, 68-9
  " Black-headed 68
  " Common 68
  " Greater Black Backed 68-9
  " Herring 68-9
  " Lesser Black Backed 68-9
Heron, Grey 35
Hobby 183
Jackdaw 22, 81, 152-5
Jay 23, 71, 118, 147-9
Kestrel 47-9
Kingfisher 14, 16, 84-5
Knot 184

Lapwing 11, 58-60, 184
Linnet 169
Magpie 71, 113, 118, 135, 140, 149-51
Mallard 10, 14, 16, 44-6
Mandarin 16, 22, 41-2, 46
Martins 98
  " House 15, 21, 90, 93-5, 102, 158, 183
  " Sand 16, 90-1, 94, 160
Merlin 183
Moorhen 10, 14, 54-6
Nightingale 17, 106
Nightjar 10, 82
Nuthatch 15, 142, 144-5
Owls 21, 112
  " Barn 77
  " Little 21, 78, 81
  " Short-eared 186
  " Tawny 14, 21, 22, 78-81
Parakeet, Ring-necked 185
Partridge, Grey 14, 51-2
  " Red-legged 50-1
Pheasant 53
Pigeon, Feral 5, 69
  " Wood 70-1
Pipits 11, 14, 96
  " Meadow 76, 96-7
  " Tree 10, 76, 96-7
Plover, Golden 184
Pochard 46
Redpoll 18-9, 162, 167, 170
Redshank 184

INDEX

Redstart, Black 186
" Common 186, 187
Redwing 108, 114-5
Robin 21, 76, 105, 133
Rook 152, 154-5
Sandpipers 16
" Common 66-7
" Green 185
Shoveler 46
Siskin 15-17, 132, 162, 167-8, 170
Skylark 11, 89
Smew 46
Snipe, Common 11, 61-3
" Great 184
Sparrowhawk 15, 47, 49, 140
Sparrow, House 11, 15, 102, 145, 158-60, 183
" Tree 14, 160-1
Starling 11, 14, 15, 21, 110, 156-8
Stonechat 187, 189
Swallow 27, 90, 92, 94-5, 98, 135, 158
Swan, Mute 4, 18, 36-7
Swift 27, 83
Teal 43, 46
Tern, Common 185
" Little 185
Thrushes 14, 15, 110, 162
" Mistle 116-8
" Song 112-3, 115, 135

Tits, Flocks of 15, 21, 132, 142, 145, 158, 160
Tit, Blue 20, 28-9, 47, 140-2, 188
" Coal 17, 132, 138-41 180, 188
" Great 15, 20, 24-7, 141 142-3, 188
" Long-tailed 136-7, 140
" Marsh 126, 138, 188
" Willow 126, 138, 188
Treecreeper 22, 144, 146
Tufted Duck 2, 46
Waders 10, 11, 14
Wagtails 11, 14
" Grey 15-6, 99
" Pied 14, 15, 99-101
" White 186
" Yellow 98-9
Warblers 11, 14, 17, 125, 129
" Garden 14, 17, 124, 126
" Grasshopper 187
" Reed 16, 188
" Sedge 16, 187
" Willow 17, 128-31
" Wood 188
Water Rail 183
Wheatear 181, 187
Whinchat 187-8
Whitethroat, Common 14, 119, 122-3
" Lesser 119-22

Wigeon 46
Woodcock 10, 19, 63-5
Wildfowl 10-1, 18, 46
Woodlark 186
Woodpeckers 15, 17, 144
" Greater Spotted 17, 87-8
" Green 86-7
" Lesser Spotted 88
Wren 22, 29, 76, 102-3
Wryneck 20, 183-4, 186
Yellowhammer 11, 176-8

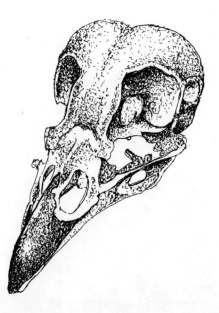

Jay's skull. Drawn by Adrian Pearsons.